How Studying Abroad Changed My Life

Mercer University expects real and tangible value for our students from their study abroad experiences. Global Education is as diverse as our student population, combining academics, research, and service in a variety of combinations and in many global locations. Student experiences abroad inform their worldview, inspiring the development of perspectives and skill sets that serve them long after they return home. This volume is a testament to the Mercer approach—one which distinguishes our educational experience.

—Felix Jelen, assistant vice president of Global Engagement, Mercer University

Global Education's power to change worldviews has long been recognized in higher education. Recently, study abroad experiences have been acknowledged for their capacity to build what is essentially a toolbox of skills that students can deploy in multiple aspects of their personal and professional life well beyond graduation. Throughout these stories you will hear students reflect on their valuable experiences abroad.

—Emily Dunn, assistant director of Global Education, Mercer University

Eminent scholars and master teachers, Drs. Houry and Obidoa draw upon their years of experience leading university-level international programs. They offer here, not a third-person primer on how to build a study abroad program, but rather a first-person testimonial as to why. In their own unfiltered voices, former students describe a compelling array of life-shaping impacts realized through study abroad. These inspiring stories will surely fuel the launch of many new international learning initiatives.

—Dr. Craig McMahan, University Minister and Director, Mercer on Mission Program

MERCER UNIVERSITY PRESS

Endowed by

TOM WATSON BROWN
and
THE WATSON-BROWN FOUNDATION, INC.

HOW STUDYING ABROAD CHANGED MY LIFE

Edited by

Chinekwu Obidoa and Eimad Houry

Foreword by

Mary Alice Morgan

MERCER UNIVERSITY PRESS
Macon, Georgia

MUP/ P717

Published by Mercer University Press
1501 Mercer University Drive
Macon, Georgia 31207

29 28 27 26 25 5 4 3 2 1

Books published by Mercer University Press are printed on acid-free paper that meets the requirements of the American National Standard for Information Sciences—Permanence of Paper for Printed Library Materials.

Printed and bound in the United States.

This book is set in Adobe Caslon Pro.

Cover/jacket design by Burt&Burt.

ISBN 978-0-88146-966-0
Cataloging-in-Publication Data is available from the Library of Congress

CONTENTS

ACKNOWLEDGMENTS

First, we wish to thank all the contributors to this book. Without your willingness and cooperation, this book would not have been possible. Your essays were a true joy to read.

Next, we acknowledge the support and encouragement of Felix Jelen, who understood the vision of this anthology effortlessly. We appreciate your swift action in helping us secure the connections necessary to move this project forward.

McKenna Kaufman was a priceless editorial assistant who took the time to read the essays and provide invaluable edits. Your fine skills helped highlight the essence of the stories here featured.

We thank Dr. Mary Alice Morgan for her willingness to contribute knowledge from many years of experience. Her contributions especially enrich this book.

Credit is due to the entire range of study abroad academic offerings at Mercer University including international exchange programs, faculty-led trips, and Mercer on Mission service programs for continuing to provide invaluable experiences for Mercer students.

Last but not least, thanks to our families, who share our love for studying abroad and have provided unwavering support to us for many years.

FOREWORD

As you read this collection of essays from Mercer University graduates who have participated in study abroad programs through faculty-led trips abroad, Mercer on Mission, Fulbright postings, the Peace Corps, or other international educational opportunities, you will learn that their experiences go beyond the excitement of traveling to new places, making new friends, eating new cuisines, practicing their foreign language skills, and encountering different cultural customs. While these kinds of experiences are part of the delights of traveling abroad, these students describe international experiences that go beyond tourism. In some cases, international travel has launched students' careers. In others, study abroad has changed their worldview. These kinds of experiences are what distinguish global education from simple "tourism."

Global education is what Mercer hopes to provide for every student, whether through semester-long study abroad courses, spring break travels, Mercer on Mission, Gilman Scholarships, our Peace Corps Prep Program, or other scholarships.

Global education enables students to go beyond the textbook study of a foreign country's history, politics, and culture to live within the interconnectedness of those factors and to realize their impact on the country. For instance, what are the ramifications of a parliamentary system compared to the US party system? Whose freedoms and rights are prioritized or marginalized in other countries? How do economies differ? For instance, is local farming being displaced by monoculture farming of a commercial crop, making farmers dependent on a global market economy? Or does a conflict like the Vietnam War continue today in the form of unexploded ordinance taking the limbs of Vietnamese farmers and their children?

As the students' essays testify, these international experiences not only broaden their understanding of other countries but also, perhaps ironically, deepen their understanding of the United States. To watch the news in a foreign country, de-centering the United States, is to experience "home" from a new and often revelatory perspective. The norms and routines of our taken-for-granted world are upended. Suddenly, our US privileges, consumption patterns, and sociopolitical structures are thrown into sharp relief, and we begin to ask new questions. For instance, why is it that many nations mandate equitable political representation of women in government or have elected female presidents, while the US does not? How can the survivors and refugees of international conflicts, such as those in Rwanda or Ukraine, be helped? What is my role in a larger world outside my town, my university, and my country?

I can tell you that from my experience leading nine Mercer on Mission trips, these are the kinds of challenging, healthy, and often heartfelt questions that Mercer students tackle during their study abroad.

So, keep reading and you will learn that Mercer not only wants every student to "major in changing the world" but also "to be changed by the world"—to become global citizens. The students here tell stories about feeling elated by their international experiences and, at other times, challenged. They talk about preparing diligently for their trips abroad, only to have the rug pulled out from under them sometimes. They tell about the process of adjusting to new living environments, food, language, transportation—seemingly everything—and using their wits and ingenuity to cope and prevail. The stories are sometimes funny and often profound. This is what I mean by transformational learning. Learning that transcends self to engender a new international self-awareness. I hope the contents of this book inspire you to become a global citizen.

—Mary Alice Morgan
Professor Emeritus,
Departments of
English and Women's
and Gender Studies;
former director,
Mercer Service
Scholars Honors Program;
and senior vice provost
for Service Learning

PREFACE

My academic journey outside my home country began in 1978 when my father decided to send me to an all-boys boarding school in Colchester, England. This was a formative experience as this small-sized school drew "privileged" students from across the globe and offered my first opportunity to compare life and experiences across borders. Upon the completion of my O-levels, I transferred to the United States to embark on my undergraduate studies. I studied business at first but found the discipline much too focused on advancing corporate interests, so I decided to switch to economics instead. I studied and wrote about the economic development of developing nations at every opportunity, which explains why I decided to pursue an interdisciplinary degree in international affairs at the master's level. With that complete, I then proceeded to complete a PhD in political science with a focus on the international political economy of democratization in emerging nations.

My first and only full-time career position as an academic began in 1991 as an assistant professor of political science at Mercer University in Macon, Georgia. Within a year of joining the department, I was summoned by the dean of the College of Liberal Arts and encouraged to seriously consider chairing the Department of Political Science the first untenured faculty to do so in the history of the college. I accepted and turned my attention to enhancing the curriculum of the program.

At the time, I became the third faculty member in the political science department and the first to focus exclusively on teaching international and comparative courses. In the year I joined, there were two internationally focused courses in the catalog: an introductory course to international relations and a comparative course on communism. Immediately recognizing the deficiencies present, I proceeded to develop a whole series of international and comparative courses over about five years. By the time the new political science curriculum was implemented in 1997, I had developed seven new courses in a variety of areas that interested me personally and that I felt would draw student interest as well.

As the variety of internationally focused courses grew, so did student interest. By 1999, I felt there was enough interest to justify the introduction of a new interdisciplinary major and minor in international affairs. I developed a multidisciplinary curriculum that incorporated internationally focused courses from nine departments in the college, making the acquisition of a proficiency level in a foreign language one of two unique features that set this program apart. The other was to require a study abroad experience, another first in the history of the college.

When I first arrived at Mercer, study abroad programs were few and far between. The university maintained exchange arrangements with institutions of higher education in a handful of countries, but, like with many other American colleges and universities, studying at Oxford was by far the most popular choice for Mercer students. Within a few years, my political science colleague Gregory Domin and I recognized the need to think more creatively and to plan programs more closely aligned with the specific courses we offered. Accordingly, the first study abroad "tour" focused on the European Union and the themes of the diffusion of authority and power. The initiative was warmly received by students, so we decided to explore other possibilities. Two more initiatives soon followed, first to Costa Rica and then to Morocco.

For all the years I have served as director of international affairs (2000 to 2023), I consistently encouraged students to spend at least one full semester abroad, preferably in a country not familiar to them. A country offering an unfamiliar culture also offers the most expansive range of learning opportunities for undergraduates trying to make sense of the world around them. Accordingly, I urged students to consider less popular destinations such as Hong Kong, Morocco, and Japan as well as less familiar parts of Western Europe such as Denmark and Sweden.

Twenty-eight study abroad programs later—to varied destinations that included South Africa, Western Europe, Costa Rica, Morocco, the United Arab Emirates, and the Republic of Georgia—I can unequivocally state that I have witnessed the transformative power of these experiences in my students.

As someone who started to study abroad as a young person, my life is a testament to the profound impact it can have. Born in Kuwait, fleeing a civil war in Lebanon, raised in Dubai, and completing my studies in the UK and the US have combined to make me the person I am and help explain my insistence on studying abroad as an invaluable formative experience. My interest in and interdisciplinary understanding of international questions, systems, and dynamics stems from these experiences. But perhaps most importantly, living in different countries and experiencing starkly different cultures in the process has transformed my worldview on a wide range of social, political, and cultural issues, allowing me to be more responsive to the needs of my students and to support them as they step out of their comfort zones.

This text aims to showcase the lasting impact of experiences abroad, from traditional study abroad programs to service-focused initiatives. The essays featured in this volume provide information on former Mercer University students and how their encounters abroad left an indelible mark on their career choices, personal lives, and worldviews.

—Eimad Houry
Former Director
of International Affairs,
Emeritus Professor
of Political Science

CONTRIBUTORS

Macire Aribot is the cofounder and co-executive director at NoirUnited International. She earned a bachelor of arts degree in international affairs and global development studies from Mercer University and a master of international affairs in economic and political development at Columbia University School of International and Public Affairs.

Alec Campbell earned a bachelor of arts in international affairs from Mercer University. He is currently serving in the military.

Anna Cizek is a cybersecurity manager at Ernst and Young. She holds a bachelor of arts degree in international affairs, global health, and French from Mercer University and a master's degree in international security from American University. She completed a Fulbright Fellowship in Morocco.

Colleen Closson is a registered nurse at the Atlanta VA Medical Center. She holds a bachelor of arts degree in international affairs and global health studies from Mercer University and a nursing degree from Emory University.

Sterling Conyers is a graduate student in global affairs at King's College London. She holds a bachelor of arts degree in international affairs and Spanish with minors in Asian studies and global health studies from Mercer University, and a master's degree in international studies from Renmin University of China.

Alyssa Fortner holds a bachelor of arts in international affairs and global development studies from Mercer University. She currently serves as a policy analyst at the Center for Law and Social Policy.

Serena Golden holds a bachelor of arts degree in international affairs and journalism from Mercer University and a master's degree in field reporting from the University of Copenhagen.

Bryant Harden is the program director of the Global Citizenship Certificate and an instructional specialist at Florida State University. He specializes in international relations and international security, with work on poststructuralist theory, modern imperialism, US development programming, and the securitization of development. Dr. Harden earned his PhD in political science from the University of Florida, an MA in international relations from the University of Warwick (UK), and a BA in political science from Mercer University.

Sarah Harris is a graduate student at the Middlebury Institute of International Studies and holds a certificate in Teaching English to Speakers of Other Languages (CELTA). She earned a bachelor of arts degree in international affairs and French with a minor in global development from Mercer University.

Amirah Houry is the director of philanthropy at BRAC, UK. She holds a bachelor of arts degree in political science from Georgia State University and a master's degree in international development and conflict from King's College, London.

Eimad Houry is a professor of political science and international affairs at Mercer University. He holds a PhD in political science with a focus on the international political economy of democratization in emerging nations. He is a seasoned teacher and winner of the 2017 Joe and Jean Hendricks Excellence in Teaching Award. He joined Mercer University in 1991 and has since developed and led or co-led twenty-eight study abroad programs of various types and lengths, more than any other faculty member in the College of Liberal Arts and Sciences.

Mckenna Kaufman is the employer engagement coordinator for Nashville International Center for Empowerment, a refugee resettlement agency. She earned a bachelor of arts degree in international affairs and journalism from Mercer University. She is also a digital media specialist based in Nashville, Tennessee, and formerly a local news reporter for Georgia Public Broadcasting.

Sophie Levelle is the chief program officer at Tandem Lab. She holds a bachelor of music in performance degree with minors in international affairs and business administration from Mercer University.

Michael Mathews holds a bachelor of arts degree in global development studies from Mercer University and is currently a graduate student at the University of Georgia.

Laurel McCormack is a child and adolescent clinician at a community health center. She earned a bachelor of arts degree in international affairs and religion with a minor in photography from Mercer University. She also holds a master of divinity from Yale Divinity School and a master of social work from the University of Connecticut.

Mary Alice Morgan has served in multiple roles at Mercer University. A member of the Department of English, she earned her BA in English from Duke University and PhD from the University of Illinois, Champaign-Urbana. She co-led Mercer's conference on W. E. B. Du Bois and co-edited *W.E. B. Du Bois and Race* (2001). Dr. Morgan served as senior vice provost for service learning for thirteen years, and during her leadership, Mercer achieved the Carnegie Classification for Curricular Engagement and Outreach and was repeatedly named to the President's Higher Education Community Service Honor Roll with Distinction. She was named a finalist for the national Thomas Ehrlich Civically Engaged Faculty Award (2013) and she received the Gulf South Award for Outstanding Practitioner Contributions to Service Learning in Higher Education (2020). In 2022, Dr. Morgan was selected for the Joe and Jean Hendricks Excellence in Teaching Award. Former chair of the Women's and Gender Studies department, she co-led eight Mercer on Mission programs to South Africa.

Chinekwu Obidoa is an associate professor of global health studies and Africana studies at Mercer University. She joined Mercer in 2013 and has been part of the Department of International and Global Studies ever since. She earned a PhD in public health from the University of Connecticut and holds master's degrees in geography, public health, and international and area studies. She is a multidisciplinary scholar with research interests in geography and health, globalization, HIV/AIDS, and the health of emerging adults. In 2017, she received the Mercer University Innovation in Teaching Award.

Anwar Parker is a psychologist and international development specialist based in Cape Town South Africa.

Hoor Qureshi is a special assistant in the Office of Public Diplomacy and Public Affairs. She holds a bachelor of arts degree in global development studies and global health studies from Mercer University and served as a Peace Corps volunteer in Botswana in 2020.

Branden Ryan is a senior gender equality and social inclusion specialist at Chemonics International. He holds a bachelor of arts degree in international affairs and Spanish with minors in history, anthropology, and Christianity from Mercer University. He also holds a master of arts degree in security policy studies (conflict resolution/gender concentration) from George Washington University. He completed a Peace Corps fellowship in Tanzania.

David Stokes is currently a youth development specialist with the Peace Corps in Morocco. He earned a bachelor of arts degree in international affairs and religion from Mercer University.

Alayna Williams is a ninth-grade teacher of multilingual learners at E. L. Haynes High School in Washington, DC. She earned a bachelor of arts degree in international affairs, Spanish, and women and gender studies from Mercer University and completed a Fulbright Fellowship in South Africa.

Chase Williams is an associate director of disaster response at GlobalGiving where he leads more than $50 million in domestic and international grant-making in support of grassroots and community-led nonprofit organizations in more than 170 countries in and after times of crisis and disaster. He holds a bachelor of arts degree in political science with minors in environmental policy and Spanish from Mercer University and a master's degree in development studies from the London School of Economics.

Tarna Zander-Velloso currently works for the US State Department as a passport specialist. She holds a bachelor of arts degree in international affairs with a minor in Spanish from Mercer University and a masters in global and international studies from the University of Salamanca.

INTRODUCTION

Studying abroad remains one of the most impactful learning experiences for students. Every year, thousands of American students participate in international educational programs.[*] What they hope to gain from the experience ranges from fulfilling academic credit to acquiring and refining language skills, broadening global awareness, and building communication competency in diverse cultural settings.[†] No doubt studying abroad holds many benefits for students; it not only enhances intellectual and academic growth, but also has a positive effect on their career, and vocational formation.[‡] Additionally, studying abroad provides opportunities for students to build transversal and life skills such as curiosity, tolerance, adaptability, and confidence. While abroad, students are exposed to a plethora of situations and contexts that catalyze change in deep and distinct ways. The emotional growth and maturity experienced can be pivotal in catalyzing change in other areas of life, including defining and redefining identity and deciding subsequent academic and educational trajectories. Research shows that students who study abroad are more likely to record postgraduation-desired milestones such as finding employment within twelve months of graduation, being

---

[*] National Association for Foreign Student Affairs (NAFSA): Association of International Educators, 2023), https://www.nafsa.org/

[†] Bain, S. F., & Yaklin, L. E. (2019). Study abroad: striving for transformative impact. Research in Higher Education Journal, 36, 1-5. https://eric.ed.gov/?id=EJ1204039.

[‡] Fry, G. W., Paige, R. M., Jon, J., Dillow, J., & Nam, K. (2009). Study abroad and its transformative power (CIEE Occasional Paper 32). Retrieved from http://www.ciee.org/home/researchpublications/documents/CIEEOccasionalPapers32.pdf

selected for their first or second choice of graduate schools, earning higher grade point averages, and earning higher salaries.[§]

While anecdotal and research-based evidence on the impact of studying abroad is well documented, how students leverage the benefits of these experiences for further growth upon return is not adequately captured or accounted for in study abroad narratives. Tips and strategies on how to navigate and maximize time abroad are ubiquitous in both personal and published sources. While being adequately armed for success is essential for every student, specific steps must be taken to ensure that the deep learning that takes place while abroad is leveraged for sustained growth and transformation years later. But how do you leverage experiences abroad for continued growth and transformation?

Post-trip reflection essays are good at capturing the effect of the experience on the student, but they can be shallow and eclipsed by the sentimental impact of the trip. Sometimes students need weeks, months, or even years to fully and adequately process their experiences and for the real power of their cross-cultural exposure to be put in perspective or even manifest.

The impact of the study abroad experience can be evaluated many years after the experience through both retrospective reflection and objective assessment of one's life journey since the experience. Using these analytical tools, the steps and strategies taken by students, directly or indirectly, to build on new insights, ideas, lifestyles, and perspectives engaged while abroad invariably emerge, revealing what is necessary for leveraging the impact for deeper and sustained positive transformation.

In this volume, we have invited alumni affiliated with Mercer University to share how their study abroad experiences shaped and transormed their lives. Here, alumni share the type of study abroad

---

[§] University of California, 2014. What Statistics Show about Study Abroad Students. https://studyabroad.ucmerced.edu/study-abroad-statistics/statistics-study-abroad.

experiences they participated in, their motivation to study abroad, the focus/topic/emphasis of their trip, duration, location, and a description of the program/s in which they participated. They share brief contextual backgrounds of the host country (geographic, cultural, political, economic, social) and how the intangible aspects of the program affected them.

Contributors were invited to revisit travel journals and reflection essays to examine how their time abroad influenced not only their academic growth and cognitive skills, but also how it affected them in general as individuals—mentally, emotionally, socially, and physically. The impact of their academic growth is explored, and the ways in which the experience informed or transformed their worldviews and perspectives are unpacked. Also, the role of the experience in shaping subsequent life decisions and trajectories is shared. Students were invited to critically evaluate their experiences, drawing both positive and negative takeaways from them.

This book includes study abroad narratives from students spanning multiple decades, academic majors, diverse career paths, and types of study abroad programs. Most Mercer alumni whose reflection essays are featured in this book graduated from the International Affairs program (IAF). The IAF program was introduced in 1999 and was the first degree program in the history of the College of Liberal Arts and Sciences to require a semester-long study abroad experience. The essays featured in this book showcase some of the legacies of this program in its twenty-five-year history.

This volume features twenty narratives from alumni and four chapters on faculty and program staff experiences in developing, designing, and executing impactful study abroad programs. The book concludes with a section showcasing tips, strategies, and recommendations for leveraging the impact of study abroad experiences for students.

Taken together, the chapters in this book highlight a somewhat neglected aspect of study abroad. It documents and shares how students build on the impact of their experiences abroad for deeper and more sustained personal and professional growth. Furthermore, it adds to the body of knowledge and literature on the impact of studying abroad on students' lives and underscores the transformational value of such experiences. Additionally, it is an important educational and pedagogical resource for professors and colleges interested in promoting and supporting study abroad in their respective institutions. It can be used as a reader for general education classes that focus on global consciousness and citizenship as well as classes that prepare students to study abroad.

The essays by no means exhaust the variety of possibilities and transformations that result from experiences abroad. However, they collectively provide a diverse and poignant array of the impact that studying abroad can deliver to students. Five domains representing five major areas of impact emerged from a close reading of the well-written and captivating stories: Purpose and Sense of Calling, New Knowledge and New Perspectives, Self-Discovery and Personal Growth, Lifestyle Change, and Critical Consciousness. The definitions of these domains are represented in the diagram at the right.[**]

[**] Graph by Dr. Chinekwu Obidoa.

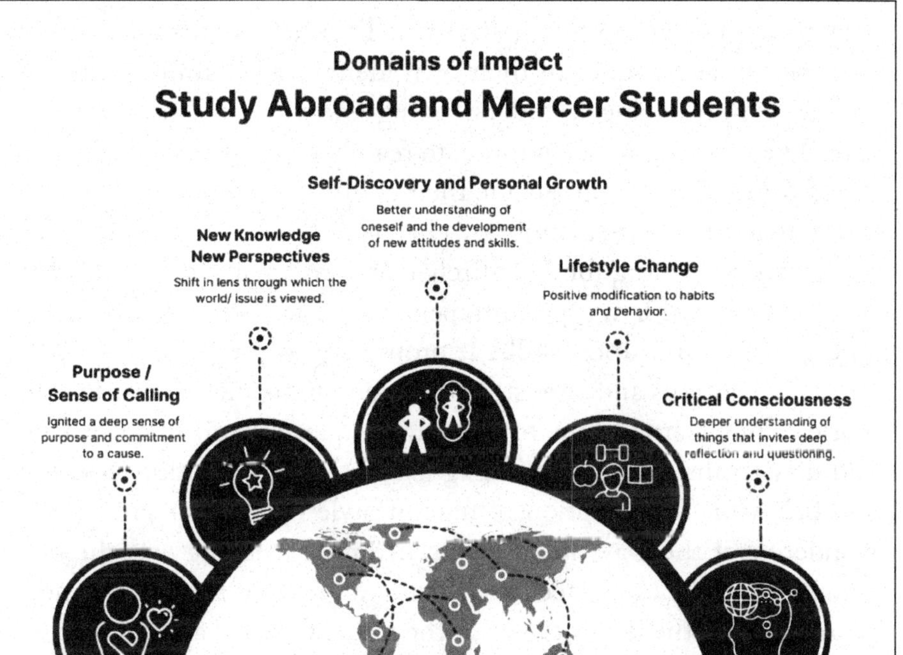
Domains of Impact
Study Abroad and Mercer Students
Self-Discovery and Personal Growth
Better understanding of oneself and the development of new attitudes and skills.
New Knowledge New Perspectives
Shift in lens through which the world/ issue is viewed.
Lifestyle Change
Positive modification to habits and behavior.
Purpose / Sense of Calling
Ignited a deep sense of purpose and commitment to a cause.
Critical Consciousness
Deeper understanding of things that invites deep reflection and questioning.

For many of the contributors, their experiences abroad fostered a deep appreciation for other cultures and human experiences they had never conceived. They shared about becoming more empathetic, self-assured, generous, open-minded, reflective, adaptable, and analytical. Also, the desire for continued personal learning and growth was evident in their narratives. Their experiences ushered in a deeper understanding of their own identity and family culture as well as a more nuanced understanding and view of American culture. They learned to listen more, to readily pivot when the occasion called for it, and to step outside their comfort zones. Their encounters abroad helped them embrace change boldly and gracefully, even if it meant retraining for an entirely new career path for some. They built and refined language, intrapersonal, interpersonal, and cross-cultural communication skills. It prompted deep reflection on preconceived notions and even stereotypes about people, places, and the world. They learned how to ask critical questions to uncover facts and new truths. Such questioning led to the modification of habits and behavior, the adoption of new lifestyle choices, or just merely wondering if the way they were accustomed to living was the best way to live. They reported recognizing a growing hunger for more knowledge on the issues to which they were exposed and an unstoppable urge to pursue greater exposure through more travel to satisfy that hunger. Finding a cause worth their commitment and dedication for the rest of their lives was another impact evident in several of the narratives; simply put, their study abroad experiences helped them find their calling and vocation. Without a doubt, the experiences abroad shared in these narratives were not only life-forming but also paradigm-shifting. We hope these stories inspire more students to study abroad, and for those who already have, not to take its impact on their lives for granted.

SELF-DISCOVERY AND PERSONAL GROWTH

1

TRANSFORMED TO TRANSFORM
HOW MY JOURNEYS ABROAD CATALYZED DEEP CHANGE IN MY WORLD

Alayna Williams

International Affairs, Spanish, Women and Gender Studies
Class of 2017

"It is better to see one time than to hear one hundred times."
—Mongolian Proverb*

At the culmination of my senior year of high school, I found myself in tears as I grappled with the decision of which college to commit to. It was May 1, 2013 (College Decision Day), and all of my friends had already signed their commitment letters, while I sat paralyzed in my high school bedroom, knowing I had only hours left to decide. Since I'd lived in Macon my whole life and had never even set foot on an airplane, I yearned for exploration. My limited travels thus far had mostly consisted of our annual family vacation to Daytona Beach, which had hardly satisfied my desire to see the world.

Part of me wanted to explore the world immediately, and in the weeks leading up to decision day, I found myself spending hours on the Peace Corps website imagining what my life in Ecuador or Morocco would be like. Little did I know how competitive the Peace Corps is. Yet another part of me wanted to stay right where I was.

---

* All proverbs used as epigaphs in this book from "Travel Proverbs from Around The World - https://passporttoeden.com/travel-proverbs/."

My family still lived in Macon, and my little sister was only six years old at the time. I couldn't bear the thought of missing her growing up.

Amidst my internal (and likely visibly external) turmoil, Mercer seemed to offer me a solution. As I sat in bed holding a Mercer on Mission brochure, I realized that I didn't have to choose between the comfort of home and international exploration: Mercer could provide me with both.

A Summer in Kerala, India

The assurance that I would be able to travel abroad at Mercer came through the Mercer Service Scholars (MSS) program. MSS is a four-year program designed for students who had been actively involved in community service during high school to continue their service work both in Macon and internationally. A hallmark of this program is university-sponsored Mercer on Mission (MOM) trip during the summer between a student's sophomore and junior year. Our MOM would take us to the enchanting state of Kerala, India. Kerala is frequently cited in books on global development and education as it boasts one of the highest literacy rates not only in India but also globally.

Our mission in Kerala was to build an aquaculture tank for Chilla, a foster home for marginalized children of sex workers, to provide the organization with a sustainable source of income. However, a couple of weeks before departing, we learned that we would also be teaching English to students at a nearby public school. While this second project was not necessarily in alignment with the sustainable, long-term impact MOMs hope to provide, being an effective volunteer means respecting and honoring the requests of community partners. So, we split up into teaching teams and began lesson planning, even though none of us were education majors.

On July 6, 2015, it was finally time to depart for our trip to Kerala. Unaccustomed to the realities of international travel, I found myself exhausted by the more than forty hours of travel it took to arrive in Thiruvananthapuram, Kerala. Once we landed, my eyes were glued to the window, as I was in awe of the bustling streets and terrified by the chaotic driving. Despite the sensory overload I experienced as someone who had never traveled abroad, as I reflect on this trip, the memory that stands out most is the moment I first entered the school where we were volunteering. The excitement and energy from the students radiated throughout the open school building, uninhibited by the walls and silence that I had come to associate with schools in the US. I felt at ease with, and inspired by, the students, most of whom were trilingual, speaking Malayalam, Hindi, and English. While we had been brought in as "teachers," the state of Kerala's commitment to literacy, and, more specifically, multi-literacy, still amazes me.

I don't know to what extent our work in Kerala changed the lives of any of the students or children we worked with, but what I do know is that the trip changed me: this trip had not satiated my desire to see the world—it sparked it.

From India to South Africa

When I arrived back at Mercer as a junior in the fall of 2014, I immediately began strategizing. *Where would I go next? Could I go somewhere for longer this time? How would I pay for it? No, really—how would I pay for it?* Soon, with guidance from my advisor, Dr. Eimad Houry, I had constructed a plan that would allow me to spend my summer in Cape Town, South Africa, with most of the trip funded by Mercer. For the first three weeks of my trip, I would participate in the faculty-led Mercer on Mission South Africa. Then I would stay behind with some of my peers for an eight-week internship at the Black Sash, a human rights NGO. To be transparent, before arriving at Mercer, I knew very little about the history of South Africa. The Eurocentric social studies curriculum I was taught as a student featured very little African history. However, as I began to learn more about apartheid, I soon realized that the racial disparities in South Africa bore a resemblance to the racial segregation I had witnessed growing up in Macon, Georgia.

Motivated to further understand the history and legacy of apartheid, I began my Mercer on Mission trip in South Africa. For this MOM, we would be coaching debate at three local schools. I volunteered at Kannemeyer Primary in the Cape Flats, an area on the outskirts of Cape Town that was once a site of forced racial segregation, one of the many grim consequences of apartheid. Nonwhite South Africans were forcibly removed from "White" areas and relocated to segregated townships like the Cape Flats. This systematic displacement disrupted families, shattered communities, and laid the foundation for immense social and economic inequality.

Despite my significant reading and research into the legacy of apartheid, I was unprepared for the harsh state of inequality in South Africa. Nevertheless, I again found myself inspired by the youth I had the opportunity to work with. At the end of our MOM, I sat in the audience with pride as the students I had coached for three weeks began their final debate. They had already won two rounds, and for the final round, one of my students, Glenda, was speaking on whether the Xhosa language should be taught in schools. She began, "If Afrikaans is taught in schools, then why should Xhosa not be taught as well?" At thirteen years old, Glenda understood the hypocrisy of teaching Afrikaans, a language spoken primarily by White South Africans.

Glenda did not win her debate that day, but her peers did begin to develop an appreciation for her culture. In the three weeks I spent at Kannemeyer Primary, it seemed that Glenda was often excluded by other students, likely because she was the only Xhosa speaker in her class. However, that day, I watched her eyes light up as her peers stomped, screamed, and chanted her name. Three weeks earlier, nearly all of the students argued that Xhosa should not be taught in schools. After hearing Glenda speak, I believe they began to question that perspective.

I walked away from that experience struck by the power of young people to serve as agents of change in their communities. While at Kannemeyer, I conducted research on teacher and student perceptions of postapartheid South Africa and was overwhelmed by the optimism and hopefulness that youth reported feeling about the country's future. I also began to truly appreciate how essential language is to identity and to question educational systems that did not foster multilingualism.

Immediately following my time at Kannemeyer, I embarked on an internship at Black Sash, an organization committed to social justice and human rights in South Africa that was originally founded as a women's anti-apartheid organization. This combination of a faculty-led Mercer on Mission and an independent internship gave me a holistic perspective on South Africa's challenges and opportunities. At Black Sash, I witnessed firsthand the impact of advocacy and community organizing in postapartheid South Africa. I saw that despite the de jure end of apartheid, the Black Sash still did tremendous work to address the racial and socioeconomic inequality the system of segregation left behind. Our work focused on supporting the organization's "Hands Off Our Grants" campaign, as the country's most vulnerable members were effectively being robbed of their grants (government-funded financial support). I had the opportunity to interview affected people and ultimately helped organize a community development workshop where more than thirty members from across the Western Cape came together to strategize how to support their respective communities. The experience solidified my commitment to service and deepened my understanding of the intricate web of social issues that needed to be addressed in the country.

To a Place of Rest

As I returned to the US and began my senior year, I knew I wanted to spend more time abroad, but I didn't yet know in what capacity. I applied to the Peace Corps and for a Fulbright scholarship to South Africa, knowing both were highly competitive. Mercer's rigorous internal process for Fulbright applicants required an interview with faculty. I still remember breaking down in ugly sobs during my interview as four professors sat across from me at a long wooden table, critiquing my personal statement. Looking back, I understand how critical that feedback process was for my personal growth, and that the professors were trying to help me craft a winning statement. Unfortunately, at the moment, I simply felt incapable of articulating how profound my experiences in South Africa had been.

The self-doubt continued as later that winter, I received an email informing me that I had been rejected by the Peace Corps. I began to doubt that my plan to live abroad would come to fruition. However, later that spring, I received the life-changing news that I had been selected as a Fulbright Scholar for South Africa.

I soon learned that I would spend my nine months in South Africa in Rustenburg, a town in the North West province that I had never heard of but whose name meant "place of rest." Initially, I was thrilled—I was going back to the country I had fallen in love with! However, in the months leading up to my departure, I allowed the opinions of others to drive me into a state of total anxiety. Much like my limited knowledge before attending Mercer, most people don't have a strong understanding of what life in South Africa is like. Therefore, many people, influenced by the crime and unrest they had seen on the news, feared those factors would define my experience. I'm disappointed to say that I let the opinions of others disrupt the prior knowledge I had gained from taking classes, writing multiple research papers, and completing a three-month internship in the country. I allowed their fears of the unknown to hold more weight than my own lived experiences. This isn't to say that there aren't real safety threats in South Africa. The legacy of apartheid has led to such profound economic inequality that violence is often prevalent. Our security briefing with the US Embassy intensified my anxiety as the list of "don'ts" was constantly growing: don't walk with your phone out, don't forget to put bags in the trunk of the car, don't drive at night, don't take an Uber, don't live in a home without security, don't roll down your windows, and so on. Ultimately, I was terrified to embark on this study abroad experience without the comfort of Mercer faculty or peers. But I decided to go anyway.

Of course, my paranoia quickly dissipated the day I stepped foot into my placement school, H. F. Tlou Secondary School. As I was introduced to the staff, I lost track of the number of times I was told, "You are welcome here" or "You are home." When I was introduced to students at a school assembly, they cheered and hollered. Some cast shy smiles and whispered suspiciously to their neighbors, while others waved frantically and shouted. I soon realized that in South Africa, my nationality and my race granted me privileges that I didn't deserve.

I spent my Fulbright primarily focused on supporting various literacy initiatives. I restored the school library and fundraised to purchase more than two hundred new books, created a library committee and book club, and provided small group tutoring for struggling readers. I also helped coach the school debate team and had a full-circle moment when my students won the debate competition for their township. It was in moments like this that I realized how well my experiences at Mercer had prepared me for working abroad. Nevertheless, when I look back now, it's not the school clubs or the projects that I remember. Those were simply vehicles that allowed me to form deep, meaningful relationships with students and teachers alike —many of whom I am still in touch with today.

Ultimately, Fulbright was the most formative learning opportunity of my entire life, and it wouldn't have been possible had I not studied abroad as an undergrad. First and foremost, the opportunity provided me with space and time to develop my personal values. When surrounded by family, friends, and the comforts of home, we are rarely challenged in our beliefs or the way we view the world. During my year abroad, I had the chance to interrogate my core values by learning from people who had experienced the world differently than I had. In this sense, I believe internships and work opportunities abroad are uniquely valuable in allowing you to experience life abroad more authentically. Furthermore, working in an international context provided me with the cross-cultural communication skills that are essential for many professional opportunities, including my current job working with students from across the world. Finally, this experience allowed me to better understand injustice, international inequality, and resistance by seeing it through the lives of my friends and coworkers. Through these experiences, I have become a more empathetic person.

Living Globally in Washington

As I reflect on my international experiences, I am most grateful for how they led me to where I am today. While my post-Mercer journey involved various detours, my passion for education, youth, multilingualism, and social justice remained consistent and brought me to my current role as a teacher of multilingual learners in Washington, DC. That said, if I could relive my study abroad journey, there are a few things I would do differently.

First, I would focus more on targeted language-learning opportunities. While my focus in South Africa was not on language acquisition, I learned only a limited amount of Tswana while there. In hindsight, *I would recommend that students think critically about language-learning opportunities before and during their study abroad experiences. If I had done so, it would have not only provided me with a hard skill to offer to future employers, it would also have allowed me to form deeper connections with my community.*

Second, I would have focused on building international connections that could have benefited me for future employment or graduate school opportunities. For example, to apply for Fulbright research grants, it is extremely beneficial to have contacts and relationships at universities abroad. Leveraging connections during study abroad can help open the door to future scholarships and opportunities.

In my current role as a ninth grade teacher of multilingual learners, I work with both long-term English learners and students who have recently immigrated to the US, primarily from Central America. My approach as an educator is informed by what I learned from students in South Africa and India; I strive to develop my students' multilingualism and elevate the lived experiences they bring to the classroom, knowing that their classmates and teachers have so much to learn from them.

My current work has also led me to reflect on how different my study abroad experiences were compared to the forced migration experiences of some of my students. While my travel was driven by a desire to explore and learn about the world around me, I always knew I could and would return home. Meanwhile, many of my students long to return to their own homes but cannot due to safety, familial obligations, or economic hardship. Their experiences have revealed what a unique privilege studying abroad is and how it should not be taken for granted. To learn from other people about their culture firsthand shapes our values and perspectives on the world. *And, perhaps more importantly, it helps us shine a light on our own culture, identity, and society, leading us to interrogate what we once considered the status quo.*

Without having studied abroad, I don't know that I would have ever thought about what it might be like to be a young person who recently immigrated to the United States. I never considered what it must be like to sit in English-only classrooms and have one of the most important aspects of your identity—your language—devalued.

And without having studied abroad, I certainly don't think I would have found my way to these students as my career. While I have always considered myself an empathetic person, there is something intangible about studying abroad that compels you to truly care about the world and those in it, and this care doesn't (or shouldn't) simply fade away when you return to the US. So, while I might not have changed the world simply by studying abroad, my world was undoubtedly transformed.

2

GROWTH AMID PAIN AND DISCOMFORT: A REFLECTION ON HOW MY STAY IN SOUTH AFRICA SHAPED ME INTO THE PERSON I HAVE BECOME

Serena Golden

International Affairs and Journalism
Class of 2021

"He who is outside his door has the hardest part of his journey behind him."
—Dutch Proverb

I nearly laughed when Dr. Houry approached me about interning at a newspaper in Cape Town, South Africa, in 2019. I longed to travel, but I was insecure, shy, and inexperienced, both as a journalist and traveler. Why would anyone believe I could handle working abroad?

I applied to the summer internship in Cape Town feeling like an imposter. Even now, I still attribute my acceptance to luck—and I am lucky because the experiences I gained that summer still shape my life today.

I had only been in the country for seven days when I was given my first assignment for Cape Community Newspapers. My editor tasked me with interviewing taxi drivers at a place called the station deck, the local term for a parking deck overrun with taxis on top of Cape Town's main station.

Taxis in Cape Town looked nothing like the yellow cabs I had seen visiting Manhattan as a child. Ramshackle white vans crammed with people sped into the Central Business District from townships outside the city. I quickly learned that taxi drivers in Cape Town are often unlicensed and operating illegally, but their services are cheap. If a resident of Khayelitsha, a western township, needed a ride into the city in search of a job, they would take a taxi.

Most of the taxi drivers refused to speak with me. I had no experience speaking Xhosa or Afrikaans, but I quickly learned that language wasn't the only barrier to communication. I was young, shy, and not from there. From my accent to my appearance, my presence didn't exactly put the drivers at ease.

Listening to a few willing interviewees, I learned that problems at the station deck were more complex than just traffic jams. At the end of the day, most of my quotes weren't appropriate for publication. According to Indian and Cape Malay drivers, Black drivers were the real source of traffic problems. It was impossible to ignore the deeply ingrained racial divisions at the station deck.

When I started my internship that morning, I had only begun to realize how much the effects of apartheid-era racial divisions lingered in South African society. The station deck broadened my context as an American who often forgets that my country's problems are not entirely unique.

That first day at Cape Community Newspapers set the tone for my summer. Traveling around the city on my own as a journalist, I was constantly throwing myself out of my comfort zone. I must have humiliated myself a hundred times, from crying on the boardwalk and asking strangers for interviews to getting lost over and over again. I also did work I'm still proud of, like producing a video about a historic neighborhood fighting to reclaim its pre-apartheid name. At the end of the summer, I said goodbye to my coworkers and the city, feeling exhausted and full of gratitude.

When I returned from Cape Town, I carried with me the lesson of diving into an unfamiliar culture with respect and humility. Reporting in Cape Town wasn't just about speaking the same words but understanding the stories, experiences, and emotions behind them. I learned to connect with people, uncover the deeper issues they faced, and tell their stories in a way that resonated with my community back home. *The ability to adapt and communicate in a foreign land is a skill I have carried with me throughout my career.*

My internship forced me way out of my comfort zone. Coming home, I felt like I could handle anything life or an employer threw at me. I knew I wanted to continue broadening my perspective and pushing the boundaries of my understanding.

Cape Town was the catalyst for a series of experiences across the globe. I delved into local journalism during the rest of my time in Macon, reporting on complex issues like youth violence in the community. I had the confidence to take on intimidating opportunities like an internship at National Public Radio. Eventually, I decided I wanted to see more of the world, and this time I did not feel like an imposter when I traveled to Europe for graduate school. I have since reported on topics like LGBTQ rights in Poland and the global movement for reproductive justice. These experiences equipped me with a broader context to comprehend and tackle issues in my own country. My journalism began to shift from local stories to those with a global perspective, and my work had a deeper purpose: to bring the world closer to the people I grew up with in Georgia.

Everything I do is bolstered by the cultural sensitivity and self-confidence I gained in Cape Town. *If there is one piece of advice I feel qualified to give, it's this: say yes to opportunities that intimidate you—in fact, actively seek them out. Your time as a student is perfect for trying new things and seeing new places with the mindset of learning more about yourself and others.*

3

UNEXPECTED: DEEP PERSONAL GROWTH IN A FARAWAY LAND

Sophie Leveille

Major: Classical Music
Minor: International Affairs, Business Administration
Class of 2018

"You will reach your destination even though you travel slowly."
—Icelandic Proverb

I came to Mercer University as a classical music major and felt lucky to receive a generous music scholarship in vocal studies. My focus leading up to college prepared me for this moment. I've been known as the "singing girl" ever since elementary school, and Mercer's program was an opportunity to solidify my interests in the field. As someone who loved business and problem-solving, I thought my most obvious route was through the music business, and I planned to double major in business in pursuit of this. After some time, my passions morphed into a fascination with law for similar reasons, with the added bonus of developing skills to build and promote compelling arguments.

As my undergraduate career progressed, I realized that most of my friends were not in music or business, but in international affairs. Encouraged by these friends, I joined an introductory class, and thus began my journey into the humanities, and later, the global affairs and social justice work I conduct now. I'd felt a palpable misalignment with my previous focus areas, not because of their subject matter, but because I felt myself itching for the "so what" of it all. Yes, I can make beautiful music, but how is *my* music driving connection and building a better world? Same for business. Yes, I was successfully learning to develop sustainable operating models, but how could *I* drive change in an increasingly divisive world? International affairs provided me with the meaning I was craving.

I grew up loving National Public Radio; it was my family's morning station of choice, and growing up in a diverse immigrant community, world issues were consistently front and center in my mind. Before entering the international affairs world, I'd thought the facts I'd learned about global affairs were best left to a future *Jeopardy* game. Being in a class centered on the facts *and* how certain watershed events had a lingering effect was a window to a new way of thinking that I was grateful to learn. I finally had a place for these previously "useless facts" to thrive and expand. These classes exposed me to opportunities where I could apply my studies in a real-life context.

On an informal basis, the International Affairs Club offered a yearly visit to Comer, Georgia, where we spent time with a former Mercer student who led the community-building efforts with the local refugee community. Many city inhabitants relocated from Myanmar following the tragic genocide of the Burmese people and persecution of their Christian population. This field trip was a unique experience. We participated in a communal church service held in one of the families' homes, were greeted with a spread of traditional foods, and were immersed in a series of intimate conversations with families in their homes to learn their stories, journeys, and the challenges they faced as refugees. Though we were in Georgia, I felt worlds away from the perspectives and comforts I was used to. This trip catalyzed a series of pivotal changes I made in my professional and academic journey.

I soon became passionate about bringing this experience to more music students at Mercer. I felt we were in a bubble regarding the impact our crafts could have; we were so focused on preserving art that we rarely had space to use it as a bridge builder. Soon after, a classmate of mine from the international affairs space program and I threw a multi-disciplinary concert bringing awareness to the refugee crisis entitled "Stateless." We called for music and art students to lend their talents to its production. The proceeds supported a community center in Comer.

The following year, I dedicated my senior project to developing a culturally competent music program for young students in Comer to promote self-expression, unity, and cultural awareness. This project brought three more music students to Comer with me to experience the community and help facilitate the program. I then began adapting the project to a study abroad context where I could focus directly on the needs of resettled youth, an approach that aligned with the students I would soon encounter in Cape Town, South Africa.

The semester preceding our immersive two-and-a-half-month experience was an intentional dive into South African culture. Our cohort participated in a class with required readings to prepare for our cultural experience, develop rapport as a group, and become familiar with the Cape Town-based professor, Mr. Anwar Parker, who would serve as our primary leader and guide in the country.

This class was necessary, given we were spending significant time abroad. We learned about topics ranging from the country's current efforts to address inequity to the national transition to democracy and modern history. Our group was diverse, so Black students like myself were prepared for the realities of living in a country that faced apartheid and the hostile attitudes we might be faced with.

In this class, participants also used this time to outline the details of their internships. I came in with the goal of testing and implementing my music program with young students ages five to nine, so my preparation primarily focused on capacity building and preparing for the school I would enter. I matched with a primary school in Mitchells Plain with a history of hosting Mercer students, and I couldn't have been more excited.

In June 2018, a few days following graduation, I began my twenty-four-hour journey to South Africa. This also marked my first trip abroad without my family.

I remember my first days in the shared house. About fourteen students shared two houses, with eight other people living in the one in which I dwelled. Outside of our preparation class, I had little interaction with my cohort. Additionally, I was the only one who had already graduated.

Reflecting on this trip, I'm surprised I did so little research on what to visit outside of my internship. Though I had a wonderful time, I wouldn't recommend this approach. I relied heavily on the research of my counterparts and, for the first month, did whatever activities they chose outside of work.

On Sundays, a few of us joined a local church, which was surprisingly similar to the services I had attended back home growing up in a Pentecostal megachurch. My biggest culture shock stemmed less from the differences and more from the unexpected similarities the culture presented. Cape Town was very modern. Many described it as the "Miami of South Africa" since it embodied a more commercialized mix of world cultures. The radio was filled with hits that I grew up listening to—Michael Jackson, Toni Braxton, and Justin Bieber filled the airwaves. Fashion was also similar. Stores were similar to those in the States. I remember feeling disappointed by this. As a musician, my biggest curiosity surrounded the music and culture, but I found it difficult to encounter local music and sounds, even though I worked in music schools and sought these things deliberately. If I were to prepare differently, I would have researched the country's musical landscape before joining the trip. I left too much of that experience up to chance. Because I was uninformed on the basics, I didn't know where to look.

Despite feeling the impact of globalization, I still took countless lessons from our free time. From awe-inspiring hikes to visits to safari sanctuaries and major landmarks like the University of Cape Town and the Rhodes Memorial, I have fond memories of the time spent in my two placements. I was first placed at Yellowwood Primary School in Mitchells Plain. Because I arrived in the winter, my internship coincided with the school's testing and break period. During this time, I faced irregular school schedules, making it challenging to fulfill my program. I was met with much larger classroom sizes than I had prepared for. Activities that could accommodate ten students with one facilitator ballooned to thirty to forty students with one or two facilitators. This challenge was compounded by the competing needs of the school—some students began preparing for their choir performances while others had playtime if they finished their work early. In short, facilitating my program became something akin to chaos. Despite everyone's best efforts, my program soon devolved into an ad hoc musical playtime.

The students were excited to play with their new American teacher, and lessons were often interrupted with requests to sing pop songs and share stories about life back home. Even writing this, I smile ruefully because at the time, I was so concerned with finishing my research I didn't fully embrace the joy around me. A major lesson I've taken from this experience is to plan small interventions. I advise others who want to launch a structured program to bring a team, or train onsite facilitators before arriving. No matter how well you plan, administering a new full-scale program alone is very challenging. Things will change, and that is okay.

As a hyper-ambitious person, my time abroad challenged my rigid understanding of productivity. The primary school was where I first encountered dedicated "tea ladies." Though this was not a formally dedicated job within schools, it was a norm in the environments I encountered. I often met women, typically older secretaries, who would check in to see if you wanted tea and a chat throughout the day. This became the highlight of many of my days, especially when I couldn't keep still amid school delays. There would be days when I would sit in the teacher's breakroom with little to do, stressing about the needs of my program or feeling unproductive. Teachers would often come to me and tell me not to worry, to enjoy the day and all that it brought. I remember feeling perplexed by the concept of "relaxing" when I wasn't fulfilling my primary duty. From this, I learned that there are greater battles, and when offered the opportunity to relax, despite my discomfort, I should take it. I am still learning that lesson, especially as I work in nonprofit settings. I often wish a "tea lady" would take my hand and offer that solace and perspective of rest.

At the school, I encountered a community artist who developed a remarkable program for youth centered around art. He'd made it his life's mission to offer a space for youth expression and positivity. His passion shone through his work, and everyone, including me, loved when he made time to teach them something. I'm thankful that we've continued to stay in touch after all these years, and he's continued to grow his nonprofit to offer art classes for students in several different townships. From him, I learned the importance of perseverance and consistency. He shared many stories about students who began to thrive in their talents after being offered a space to create. He taught me how important it is to meet students where they are. Though his primary role was art teacher, he knew some students came to his class because he supplied snacks and food. He served them without hesitation and offered the space for them to create if they wished.

I took on a teaching assistant role in a Grade 0 (kindergarten) class to fill the time between my music classes. I loved my time in the classroom, surrounded by students and their curiosity. As in my music classes, the students were fascinated with my Americanness.

One day, we had spare time in class, so the teacher allowed me to lead a question-and-answer session with the students. I was struck when one of them, at such a young age, asked about the violence in my country; the Coloured township where this school is located is overrun by gangs and violence.

Once the primary school went on break, our program leader found a second placement for me to spend the remainder of my time in Cape Town. As a recent graduate, I was set to start a guest lectureship at a preparatory music institute closer to the city with an older age group. Students here ranged from sixteen to twenty. I was a twenty-one-year-old coming from a very different background. Given my educational expertise, I began teaching musicianship and music theory classes for their earliest levels and soon moved into the songwriting and music business. This experience taught me how much more I enjoyed working with older students and how much further our conversations could go. We formed a sense of camaraderie and made tremendous memories through our class and the local activities we participated in during our lunch breaks. Through this placement, I was finally exposed to local music and art. This was a tremendous personal celebration.

Our conversations about American culture were far less dream-like than with the kids in primary school. There were the expected misconceptions about the level of affluence people had on average, but I was surprised to learn how much more they knew about my culture than I did about theirs. This is understandable in many ways, but it was interesting to experience firsthand.

My biggest learning in this placement stemmed from facing my privilege as a US-born person. I had to check my authority several times. Yes, I was knowledgeable about music, but I became increasingly aware of how much my Americanness seemed to give me unearned credibility. This realization made me aware that less thoughtful approaches could easily go unchecked and that foreigners could inadvertently assert power over others. *I advise people entering situations of power to check themselves consistently. Sometimes you can overstep and need to shift authority back to experts, whether present or not.*

I could go on and on about the lessons I took from my study abroad experience, and reflecting on the effect these experiences have had on my current life is profound. I feel a deep connection to South Africa and a kinship with the people I encountered. I am grateful that I expanded my network to include people who have different perspectives and backgrounds from mine. The experience helped solidify my next steps after graduation and offered me an opportunity to try my hand at program development, lecturing, and practicing culturally competent communication. I continue to apply these skills to my work today.

Through my deepened exposure to different cultures, assessment of my skills and talents, and realignment with my values, I've reshaped my journey to focus on developing a more unified and intentional world. I don't insist that this is everyone's path, but I hope others can take the journey to discover their path through these experiences.

Since I participated in this program, I've continued to utilize the skills I picked up. I've entered situations more curious and learned how to be more resourceful and intentional as I develop relationships with people who are seemingly unlike me. Most profoundly, I look beyond backgrounds to draw on shared perspectives as a point of connection. This is something I encourage many to do, and this made my work in fundraising and program development much more successful and fulfilling. I've come to view the activities associated with "making a connection work" as necessary puzzles rather than unapproachable obstacles. In addition to developing this refined knack for finding throughlines, I became much more practiced in my ability to be scrappy. Working in small schools and centers translated perfectly to my work developing a community center and in startups when we needed to pivot quickly and adapt available resources. Most notably, this experience validated my entrepreneurial spirit. It was a valuable experience learning how receptive people were to my ideas and to see a program or lesson I dreamed up come to fruition.

I would advise students who are interested in studying abroad to:

• Assess the opportunities presented and make sure you're choosing an experience that cuts to the core of the growth you want to make, but not get too stuck on what that should look like. Every experience is different, every culture offers different lessons, and no trip will be exactly what you expect. There's no way to make a perfect choice, but I approached my Cape Town trip with a desire for a deep immersion into a new culture, exposure to different settings, and the opportunity to work with children. I was able to fulfill each of these wishes and more. By keeping my expectations vague, I was able to allow the experience to shape around me. As I mentioned earlier, my initial desire to work with children was adjusted, and I was able to work with an age group better suited to my interests.

• Hold on to your assumptions about a country's culture loosely before experiencing it yourself. Though it's important to prepare yourself for possible inequity and discrimination, if I'd insulated myself too much out of fear, I would have missed out on a lot of amazing opportunities. I found that people were kind, open to conversation, and acted "normal" despite my "otherness." I think it's also important not to ostracize the people you're encountering by asking possibly insensitive questions about their lived experiences in the wrong context. As I mentioned earlier, these experiences are reciprocal, and pressing for answers is not the way to develop relationships or gather honest accounts. It just makes people uncomfortable, so be mindful.

My studies abroad offered me an immersive opportunity to move out of my comfort zone and live out new perspectives in real time. I credit this experience with helping me to develop my courage, ability to pivot quickly, and ability to laugh through trying work situations. In addition, I made cherished memories that I carry with me to this day.

4

FOUR COUNTRIES, THREE CONTINENTS: A JOURNEY OF SELF-DISCOVERY

Sterling Conyers

Majors: International Affairs, Spanish
Minors: Asian Studies, Global Health
Class of 2018

"Traveling thousands of miles is better than reading thousands of books."
—Chinese Proverb

Upon arrival at Mercer University, I was unsure about which discipline I wished to commit to for the next four years. Potential career paths danced in my head, from continuing ahead with the Spanish language and finding work as a translator to abandoning the humanities entirely and trying my hand at something new. The exact details regarding how I decided to declare a major in international affairs have blurred with the years; all I can say is that by the end of my freshman year, I found myself signing the form in Dr. Houry's office and submitting it to the registrar next door. Little did I know that a pair of signatures would alter the trajectory of my life and impart such richness to my lived experiences to come.

China

The first departure from my loosely constructed pre-Mercer five-year plan involved continued European language study. Having devoted five years to Spanish throughout middle and high school, I planned to begin studies in German as well, expanding beyond the Romance language family. Content to continue deepening my understanding of Spanish, I was in the midst of preparations for the language placement exam when I was approached by my advisor and presented with the idea of studying Mandarin Chinese. Apart from a brief interest in Japanese during my adolescence, I had never considered or even imagined the prospect of Asian language study since my school offered only French and Spanish. Out of curiosity more than anything, I registered for Beginning Mandarin, taught by longtime Mercer professor and resident saint Miao Marone. Over the next year, I would attend class four days each week to engage in speaking practice, complete listening exercises, and develop familiarity with Chinese syntax. To this day, I have yet to study anything quite like it; the absence of any alphabet, four separate tones, and more than four thousand years of constant cultural evolution alongside the language render the attainment of fluency in Mandarin a never-ending, consistently thrilling quest.

Halfway through the year, Professor Marone announced that she would be leading a study abroad trip to China, where students would be enrolled in Chinese courses at the renowned Nanjing University, located in the former southern capital of Nanjing. She emphasized the importance of being able to experience, speak, and respond to the language within the context of a fully immersive environment, replete with Chinese sociocultural customs and daily interactions. It seemed an opportunity too rare to pass up—the chance to visit China, despite not speaking fluent Mandarin, with a professor I adored and to learn more about a language I had spent the better part of the year growing more excited about with each class.

We set about accumulating the veritable pile of documents required to apply for a Chinese tourist visa, including a record of accommodations, flight confirmation, and passport information. After several emails, meetings, and discussions about the itinerary, it was suddenly the morning of May 31st and I was heading to the Atlanta airport. After a short flight to Chicago, we were on another, much larger plane bound for Shanghai. Despite the subarctic temperatures of the air conditioning, which persisted relentlessly throughout the flight, I gazed out the windows during my waking moments and tried to imagine the cities, people, and knowledge awaiting us on the other side of the world as we hurtled through the sky.

Once we landed in Shanghai and cleared customs, the first thing I noticed about China was the sheer number of people everywhere. With the third largest population in the world, at nearly twenty-five million people, Shanghai boasts the largest population in the country. Sidewalks as wide as highways were flooded with never-ending streams of people, including the employed, the unemployed, children, the elderly, and street vendors. Each McDonald's, which I was surprised to see so far from home, was three stories tall. From the view of our hotel room, the city seemed to stretch forever in every direction. The next three weeks passed in a blur of historic sights and unfamiliar sounds. The university held courses on Chinese food culture and calligraphy. Professor Marone hustled us from landmark to landmark, including Zhongshan National Mountain Park and Xuanwu Lake. While living there, I observed many things during our unhurried moments. Our teacher, a student studying education at Nanjing University, stood respectfully each time Professor Marone entered the room. Hand-waving was scarce, locals preferring instead to nod as a form of greeting. It was safe to walk anywhere, even at night. Vendors encouraged bargaining, but we spoke so haltingly that our money was snatched and change placed in our hands before we could blink. There was always sound, whether from a group of elders dancing in the park, the speakers blasting outside a shop downtown, or the dedicated whir of the scooters whizzing down the streets. Almost everywhere we went, eyes followed our path: some subtle and some blatant.

As our classes proceeded, it became evident just how much Chinese there was to learn and how little of it we had mastered in a single year. Ordering food was a challenge that involved lots of pointing and intense examination of any accompanying photos; we became accustomed to eating whatever arrived. There, we learned the wonders of the lazy Susan table, a rotating table that grants each person a chance to help themselves to a plethora of steaming-hot dishes.

I found myself mellowing with the days and taking any opportunity to speak with the locals we came across, many of whom were excited to help. During a conversation with friends, I remember asking our host what his life goal was. "To be happy every day," he replied.

I was struck, perhaps belatedly, that this simple phrase echoed and reflected the aspirations of so many; that we, on every corner of the globe, exist for the pursuit of happiness to varying degrees, and that differences in language, phenotypes, and location cannot obscure the basic essence of humanity we all possess. It wasn't that I realized the humanity of our hosts that day, but rather that I recognized the connection we all share and the duty we have to our fellow man in acknowledging that humanity and maintaining a sense of morality throughout our interactions with one another. My time in China solidified my desire to deepen my Mandarin language studies and gave me a precious glimpse of life beyond the borders of my home country.

Dubai

Six months later, another opportunity arrived. Dr. Eimad Houry announced that he was embarking on his yearly faculty-led study abroad trip to Dubai, one of the seven United Arab Emirates, and he encouraged us to participate. Located on the Arabian Peninsula, Dubai is world-renowned for its innovative architecture, dedication to luxury, and commitment to modernizing the desert landscapes it inhabits. It is also known for utilizing cheap migrant labor to support ongoing construction, domestic workers, and professional expats, who fill many white-collar jobs.

Once the flight landed, we enjoyed a meal of food typically enjoyed around the Mediterranean and the Arab world: falafel, hummus, and endless tins of hot fries. The rest of the week consisted of visiting the Burj Khalifa, which remains the world's tallest building, a desert safari adventure, trips to the spice souk, and more. While a significant proportion of publicly available knowledge about Dubai focuses on its wealth, as well as the glitz and glam this wealth cultivates, Dr. Houry intentionally planned events and activities that were not touristy, giving us opportunities to gain a deeper understanding of the lives of the Emirati men and women from the region, as well as the many migrants working there.

Personally, one of the most meaningful activities of our week in Dubai was a religious visit to a mosque, where we enjoyed a traditional meal, learned Islamic customs, such as washing oneself before entering a mosque, and were given the opportunity to ask locals questions about life in Dubai. We asked to what extent they felt religious beliefs influenced their quality of life in Dubai, and whether Islam was seen as empowering for local women. Our guide praised the freedom she experienced in Dubai and cited the attainment of her degree as evidence that women could reach the same heights as men, despite negative assumptions in the West.

My favorite activity of the entire week was sharing dinner with Dr. Houry's extended family, who generously opened up their home to us and provided snacks, entrees, and dessert for the group. Before traveling to Dubai, I had been ignorant of both Arab and Muslim customs but learned throughout the trip that the religion highly prioritizes the duty one has to guests and one's fellow man in general. The third pillar of Islam involves the obligation of any Muslim to offer charity from excess wealth, and those we encountered exhibited this throughout our stay. Dubai made me aware of the innovation and ingenuity of humankind, emphasized the importance of harnessing local resources to promote environmental preservation, and deepened my understanding of the Islamic religion, its teachings, and the importance of these teachings to the moral tenets of its believers.

South Africa

The next opportunity announced by the International and Global Studies program called for interns to apply to summer programs of their choice in South Africa, the rainbow country. South Africa is a nation with a complex colonial history that is still grappling with postcolonial machinations and a gross imbalance of wealth distribution to date. I packed my bags and headed for Hartsfield Jackson's international terminal to board what remains the longest flight of my life, and one of the longest nonstop flights in the world: the distance from Atlanta, Georgia, to Johannesburg, South Africa, measures approximately 8,425 miles and between fifteen and seventeen hours, depending on which direction you're flying.

Upon arrival, we interns had the chance to participate in excursions planned for the Mercer on Mission group, whose time there overlapped with ours. South Africa echoed the state of race relations that existed domestically in the wake of the post-Civil War South, Reconstruction, the Jim Crow era, and the Civil Rights Movement, and for that reason felt eerily familiar. Drives around Cape Town displayed the wealth disparity between the coast and the inland areas, directly reflecting apartheid-era segregation. During the first few weeks, we visited museums and historic sites around Cape Town that memorialized this history, showing how Dutch and English colonial powers exploited local resources and controlled the movement of Black and Colored peoples during apartheid.

Our internships began in mid-June and lasted until August. My internship, for Cape Community Newspapers, taught me the art of clear and concise journalistic writing and how to focus on overarching themes in the composition of an article. The team leader assigned me as a photographer to a journalist reporting on issues affecting the Coloured community. Though I was not responsible for conducting interviews, I photographed the subjects and their surroundings for the newspaper. I was allowed to listen to the concerns weighing on the hearts of those interviewed, to hear their worries about community safety and education, and to witness those motivated enough to make a difference. The role that media consumption plays in opinion-forming and stoking or encouraging solidarity amongst community members cannot be understated. It was a privilege to watch and emulate coworkers diligently double-checking their sources, following up in person and over the phone, and making trips out to the field to witness the news stories for themselves. The reporting team embodied Cape Community Newspapers' dedication to serving as a reliable primary and secondary source of Cape Town-relevant information. Though the scope of this reporting occurred on a local level, the sociohistorical effects of globalization, both negative and positive, color and influence each interaction in Cape Town.

Morocco

The spring of my junior year represents the culmination of my study abroad experiences at Mercer. Initially, I planned to study in England, but Dr. Houry suggested instead Al Akhawayn University in Ifrane, Morocco. Citing England's cultural similarity to the USA, he questioned why I would choose a destination without a language barrier if I could challenge myself by studying in a comparatively unfamiliar locale. I considered the religious and demographic differences between the UK and Morocco, the federalist system in place on United States soil versus the unitary monarchy maintained in Morocco. It was evident that Morocco possessed a competitive advantage over England in terms of dissimilarity to my home country and the potential for unprecedented experiences, so I was off to

Casablanca in early January of 2017 for the longest length of time I had spent away from home. Located around five thousand miles above sea level, Ifrane was difficult to access. Another flight to Fes and a subsequent taxi ride later, we slipped over the days-old ice and snow toward our accommodation, the newest and coldest residences of Ifrane. The first few weeks were maybe the coldest I have ever been on this planet—nighttime temperatures hovered near 0 degrees Celsius—so suited and booted, we shuffled from building to building for orientations, activities, and introductory lectures. The week after we arrived, the local students returned to the school for the semester to begin.

They call Morocco, colloquially, the land of schizophrenia, referring to the amalgamation of colonial histories and languages that have made their impact on the nation as a whole. The average Moroccan attendee of Al Akhawayn University spoke a minimum of three languages—Darija (Moroccan-dialect Arabic), French, and English—and constantly switched between them in casual conversation. My classmates discussed whether Moroccans were considered Arab, as the architecture and state religion suggest. As members of the MENA region, one might think so, but a consensus does not exist; questions of identity are sensitively and frequently posed. Moroccans are descendants of North African aboriginal tribes who share ancestry with colonial occupiers such as the Arab, French, and Spanish peoples. Having next to no knowledge about Morocco before I arrived, the immersion of taking classes at Al Akhawayn meant I learned fairly quickly.

The unforgiving weather and constant snow meant I spent most of the winter on campus. A full course load had the majority of us permanently seated in computer labs or at library tables, keeping up with our homework and prepping for assessments. One of my favorite courses that semester was Women in Islam. In the first class, students had the opportunity not only to learn more about Islam as a religion but also to critically analyze it from a feminist perspective.

We studied prominent Moroccan authors such as Fatema Mernissi, a twentieth-century sociologist recognized for her texts on women, gender, and the feminine experience. Having been raised a Christian Baptist, these classes were invaluable to me and further outlined the universality that threads through accounts of womanhood worldwide.

Although my four-month stay was nothing like I expected, it was everything but forgettable. Outside of the academic responsibilities, I discovered the well of resilience I held within myself. The curiosity that propelled me to discover as much as I could about my environment abroad in turn informed my journey to self-discovery. Throughout the semester, I was able to cultivate friendships and make memories I will hold dear for the rest of my life. Morocco further developed within me a sense of spontaneity and a greater appreciation for the chance to see the world.

All told, throughout my academic career at Mercer, I participated in four study abroad opportunities in China, Dubai, South Africa, and Morocco, respectively. I am infinitely grateful to those who advocated for and facilitated these opportunities for me. These were journeys I embarked upon for the sake of knowledge enhancement and self-exploration.

During the completion of courses for international affairs, I studied subjects like international conflict and security, the politics of developing nations, epidemiology, and medical sociology. It is easy, especially as a privileged resident of the United States, to feel disconnected from the lives of those examined in case studies or referred to in textbooks. The portrayal of these people, even in documentaries or through primary sources, is insufficient to communicate the nuanced reality of their lives. Studying abroad, however, is full of moments that reinforce the importance of intercultural understanding and communication, skills that can only deepen with time and effort. Traveling, honing language skills, sightseeing, and prioritizing communication with the locals are some of the many ways to maximize your time abroad. Taking classes abroad in subjects that interest you can present similar information from different perspectives and cultural contexts.

If I had any advice, cliché though it may be, I would advise against being afraid to try new things or challenge your worldview. Attempt to look at things from diverse perspectives and viewpoints. Interactions with the economically disadvantaged or politically disenfranchised moved me, further confirming the study of international affairs as necessary to the pursuit of my aspirations in life. Throughout my travels, I was committed to posing questions whenever possible, to professors, employees, and friends. The importance of approaching new situations with an open mind, a neutral outlook, and a positive attitude cannot be understated.

I'm sure on your walks around Mercer's beautiful campus, to and from Knight Hall, past Groover, and along the path bordering the University Center, you've seen the banners waving gently in the wind, displaying the saying, "Everyone majors in changing the world." Studying abroad is unique in that it grants you the opportunity to come across people you certainly would not have met otherwise—people with separate perspectives, opinions, and decisions informed by their respective sociological factors, common language(s), and politics.

Study abroad opportunities grant participants access to broader and more forgiving perspectives—of the inequalities that affect all of us, the histories we share, and our roles as members of a global community. It reveals who we are and what we value outside the scope of nationwide societal norms. Self-exploration and self-awareness create well-rounded and measured individuals, equipped with the motivation and resolve necessary to major in changing the world.

5

FROM PERSONAL GROWTH TO FINDING MY PASSION: HOW MY TRIP TO SOUTH AFRICA SHAPED MY CAREER TRAJECTORY

Tarna Zander-Velloso

Major: International Affairs
Minor: Spanish
Class 2019

"If you love your son, let him travel."
—Japanese Proverb

I am a person of Brazilian heritage. In the summer of 2018, my junior year as a new Mercer University transfer student, I participated in one of the most rewarding experiences of my undergraduate career—a three-week trip to South Africa with Mercer on Mission (MOMSA). I had entered Mercer the semester prior as an excited but unsure transfer student who had overcame difficult personal and health challenges to continue college at a new school. As I worked to rebuild my confidence in an academic setting, MOMSA improved my self-assurance and taught me to view international affairs from a deeper perspective. This unique program, organized by the international affairs department, combined academic classes, service work, and cultural immersion. As I directly engaged with the people and culture of Cape Town and the surrounding townships, I wrestled with difficult questions about violent protest, educational failures, responsible water use, corporal punishment, and ethical tourism.

The rigorous academic portion of the program, which focused on the complex challenges faced by the country in addressing the historical legacy of apartheid, prepared me and my twelve classmates for our time in Cape Town. Our classes forced us to think critically about the connection between past and present longstanding issues such as national identity, crime, gender violence, poverty, and public health. The challenges that stood out to me were the ones that focused on the nation's transition to constitutional democracy, the commitment to a "Rainbow Nation" united by diversity, socioeconomic inequality rooted in the apartheid system, and the country's educational initiatives.

Our academic journey continued even after we arrived in Cape Town, with classes taught by a University of Cape Town professor and informal gatherings with his students. Weekly journals assigned for homework taught me to think deeply about my daily experiences and how they connected to what I had learned in classes. Unforgettable cultural experiences enhanced our learning and included excursions to iconic places such as Table Mountain, Robben Island, Cape of Good Hope, Iziko Slave Lodge, District Six Museum, Kirstenbosch National Botanical Gardens, the colorful neighborhood of Bo-Kaap, traditional artisan markets, a wildlife safari, and a local winery. Both the academic and cultural elements of the program were incredible, but the service component of MOMSA was what originally caught my eye and inspired me to apply. Education was especially important for all of us in the program because our service work was based in primary and secondary schools in Khayelitsha, one of the largest townships in Cape Town.

In the mornings, I worked as a teaching assistant in a primary school, while in the afternoons I moved to a secondary school to help train students for their first-ever Model United Nations conference. The educational service component of Mercer on Mission

South Africa was the most transformational part of the study abroad experience for me because it was the first time that I had taught or mentored students. My time with my students reinforced how much I value the pursuit of education.

The students I worked with were smart, inquisitive, creative, and had endless enthusiasm for learning. Even in the face of structural inequality and historical barriers, the power of education in their community and their enjoyment of learning was undeniable. They taught me just as much as I taught them, and probably even more so. I learned more about local cuisine when I tried one of their favorite recess snacks, chicken feet. I learned how to manage uncomfortable conversations when a discontented high school student in our Model UN program asked me point-blank, "Why are you even here?" I learned how to think on my feet as I improvised a Spanish lesson to calm a rowdy, thirty-five-person class. I learned the importance of unconditional kindness as I watched my younger students' engagement in the class grow when I complimented their artistic doodles. Two of my biggest takeaways was learning the power of sharing my passions (soccer, international affairs, and Spanish), while actively embracing the passions of my students.

To my surprise, my Khayelitsha students inspired me to explore opportunities to make an educational impact in the local community around Mercer when I returned from South Africa. The global engagement of MOMSA made me aware of how American society, in focusing on "helping" communities abroad, often fails to address inequalities at home. It opened my eyes to the fact that even though Cape Town is on another continent, across the Atlantic, and in another hemisphere far away from Macon, both cities share similar challenges in terms of the experience of minority communities. These realizations led me to discover Upward Bound, a federal TRIO educational program that works to empower students disproportionately affected by structural inequalities.

The Mercer University office of the organization aims to motivate and prepare high school students who are underrepresented in higher education due to their families' educational and financial backgrounds. I first worked for the organization as an after-school English tutor while at university, preparing students for the ACT exam. Immediately after graduating, I joined the summer program team as a full-time tutor counselor, where I had responsibilities as an English teaching assistant, an MLA writing tutor, and a dormitory supervisor. As with MOMSA, my time with the students was my favorite part of this work. Their passion, intellect, humor, and diverse personalities made every day exciting. I was constantly challenged to keep adapting to their interests and needs. When the summer program ended and I found myself rejected by the international relations fellowships that I had applied to, I realized that the field of international education was the perfect option that was staring me in the face—especially with the advantages of having my previous experiences in Cape Town and Macon. Through a combination of luck and fate, I found a teaching program in Spain called the North American Language and Culture Assistants Program (NALCAP/*auxiliaries de conversación*) on a Mercer fellowship and job email list. After talking with one of my Spanish professors whose son had participated, I decided to apply because it seemed like the ideal next step to make the most of my international affairs and Spanish studies, teaching experience, and my desire to work before deciding on graduate school options.

My time as part of MOMSA was crucial in motivating me to embark on the journey after getting accepted into the program. Since Cape Town was the first place I lived without my parents, MOMSA gave me a preview of living independently as an adult and making my own decisions. The Mercer on Mission South Africa experience reminded me of all the reasons I love to travel and showed me all the profound connections that can be made when you visit a place you have committed to learning about extensively beforehand.

One major insight MOMSA provided me is that over time I have grown more independent, more willing to take on challenges, and better able to integrate my academic learning with personal experience. It also confirmed my belief that I am happiest when I am traveling. Moving to Spain only further justified that sentiment. Though I had only planned to participate in NALCAP for one school year, after being placed in a secondary school in the community of Castilla y León, I ended up renewing my contract during the COVID-19 pandemic and later completed a two-year master's program at the University of Salamanca. Spain has given me more than I could have ever imagined, from living with a Spanish host family in Valladolid and gaining firsthand insight into the public school system to finally speaking Spanish fluently with a fairly decent accent. I also had the opportunity to teach English at a local language academy, travel around the country as an assistant soccer referee for women's second division meet new friends from numerous countries, appreciate centuries of incredible history, and write a master's thesis. I can say that I have fallen in love with many facets of living in both Spain and Europe despite periodic headaches with the bureaucratic process of working abroad and navigating cultural differences. There was a time when I could not envision myself living in a foreign country upon graduation, so I credit the well-organized structure and reach of MOMSA for helping me make the most of my love for international learning and inspiring me to take that passion to the next level.

A life lesson that I took away from MOMSA is that journaling and writing do wonders for the mind and soul. For me, the practice is crucial from both a personal and academic standpoint. I recall that on the initial flights from Atlanta-Amsterdam and Amsterdam-Cape Town, I spent hours handwriting my first journal entry for our course (even though the assignment was relatively simple: just yourself and your motivation for deciding to embark on the trip). Though I had kept travel journals for many years and had started a daily journal fairly recently, I jumped at the new opportunity to embark on a more analytical writing project. The activity was not only therapeutic, it forced me to purposefully document my thoughts and learning experience as a whole. For example, in moments of discomfort when I felt like I was intruding as an outsider in the townships, a place where I did not belong, the journal allowed me to reflect on why I thought that way. It allowed me to draw from my lessons on South African history and my own beliefs to address complex situations I found myself in. I learned that journaling could be more powerful than I had ever imagined.

My trip abroad to South Africa shaped my career trajectory by inspiring me to join the educational field as a teacher with Upward Bound and to work in the region of Castilla y León, which was something I had never considered before. In Spain, I had the pleasure of working with numerous families, children, and adults in private classes. Many Spaniards place a very high value on learning English as part of belonging to a global society, which made it exciting to be an active part of language and cultural exchange with my students.

If I could change something about MOMSA if given the chance, I would have done a better job staying in touch with my fellow participants and my professors after the end of the program and after graduation.

6

CROSSING CULTURES, BEYOND BORDERS: LESSONS IN ADAPTABILITY, RESILIENCE, AND RESOLVE

Branden Ryan

Majors: International Affairs and Spanish
Minors: History, Anthropology, and Christianity
Class of 2013

"Traveling is a return to the essentials."
—Tibetan Proverb

It was July 2017. I stared out of my car window at the rolling hills, dust kicking back from the tires and blanketing my view. A dry desert extended in front of me, leading out from the Singida region up through Shinyanga, a city in northern Tanzania. This trip represented the culmination of my experiences as a Peace Corps volunteer. I had arrived in Tanzania in July 2013, just months after graduating from Mercer University, to embark on two years of service. Two yearlong extensions later, I found myself traveling between different villages throughout Tanzania, cutting across the countryside to conduct site visits where Peace Corps volunteers led menstrual hygiene management interventions to support secondary school girls. Each ride and visit turned into a new mirror allowing me to reflect on my time in East Africa. After arriving in Shinyanga, checking into my modest hotel, and grabbing dinner, I settled in to check email, send off a few site visit summary reports, and upload photos and videos documenting the impact of the interventions on girls' lives. I opened my inbox and found an email titled "Mercer Development Summit—Invitation to Speak" from a Mercer staff member. Just four years out from my undergraduate experience, I felt honored to accept the invitation.

In October of that same year, I watched as students, faculty, and community members began pouring into Willingham Auditorium. Never one to shy away from an opportunity to speak publicly, I still found my palms sweaty as I sat onstage, peering out toward the audience while exchanging a few pleasantries with my co-speakers. When it was time, I stepped up to the lectern, looked out, and shared one of my favorite personal sayings I have relied on throughout my career as an opening statement: *always trust your guts, but not your farts*. The audience giggled in response, and I smiled in return, knowing that the rest of my speech would go off without a hitch.

As I reflected on my Mercer experience in Willingham Hall four years postgraduation, I was struck by how my five-month exchange program in Hong Kong had seamlessly linked my undergraduate life to my career in international development. My father worked for the US Army at the NATO base in the Netherlands, and I remember, as a child, being intrigued by the eclectic mesh of cultures of my fellow students at the international school where most of our parents had similar placements. Living in this intercultural setting exposed me to a unique blend of worldviews, sharpened my intercultural skills, and opened me to a world of possibilities. Unsurprisingly, at Mercer I graduated with a double major in international affairs and Spanish with minors in anthropology, Christianity, and history to satiate my appetite for world politics, history, culture, and languages. When I left for Tanzania after graduation, a sense of nostalgia returned.

A life that was built on my ability to adapt to different cultures, required me to rethink my notions of international development at a community level, and allowed me to build friendships with my community members by teaching more than fifty hours a week and facilitate gender empowerment, HIV/AIDS, malaria, and leadership education sessions. And most importantly, a life that was marked by new exploration, growth, and inspiration.

What I often exclude from that narrative, though, is my five-month study abroad in Hong Kong during the spring semester of my junior year. Though my time in Hong Kong represents a small section of my life's tapestry, the threads that link my childhood to my Peace Corps experience and now my fulfilling career in international development all pass through this semester.

Lesson 1: The Art of the Pivot

In December 2011, as a junior at Mercer University, I was planning how to fulfill the study abroad component of my international affairs degree. My choice to study abroad in Hong Kong was quickly rewarded. The semiautonomous city-state's history, straddling the legacy of the British Empire and the People's Republic of China and its strategic location as an international transport and business hub, created a vibrant mix of history and modernism. Indeed, life in Hong Kong was certainly more dynamic and fast-paced than life in Macon and required adaptability, patience, and perseverance. From figuring out how to use the public transport system, navigating cultural etiquette and faux pas to finding innovative ways to cook limited groceries on induction stoves in unfamiliar communal kitchens, one thing about a study abroad experience is that it requires a lot of self-motivation and curiosity. Had I not been open to studying at Hong Kong Baptist University (HKBU)—a place where I had little familiarity, no language ability, and little knowledge about the full historical or cultural context—I would not have had the opportunity to see how adaptable, flexible, and independent I was by the end of my study abroad experience.

My adaptability and flexibility were tested during my senior year at Mercer. In April 2013, I faced a critical juncture: pursue a master's degree in Washington, DC, or embark on a two-year teaching journey abroad with the Peace Corps. With my Spanish major, I was sure my Peace Corps placement would be somewhere in Central or South America, and I dreamed of the fluency I would have after speaking Spanish daily for two years—especially after it suffered from my one semester in Hong Kong. When the email finally arrived, I took a deep breath to quiet the mix of anticipation, dread, and excitement and clicked on it. I didn't even read the introduction before scrolling down to see TANZANIA, SECONDARY EDUCATION (ENGLISH) in large, bold letters. Jaw open, that deep breath quickly exited in a shocked gasp. East Africa? I had told the placement officer that I preferred somewhere I could put my Spanish to use, but that I would be flexible. Well, this was certainly a flexibility exercise, and in the spirit of adventure (slightly mixed with resignation), I looked at this assignment as an opportunity to grow intellectually and socially.

The "art of the pivot" is not just an action, but a philosophical way to consider new opportunities. If anything, my experiences have taught me that academic and professional progression is not always linear. If you had asked my freshman self whether I would have studied abroad in Hong Kong or lived in Tanzania for almost five years after graduation, that version of me might have laughed. But rather than going through the first door that presented itself, I soon realized that there were doors all around me that offered new, unexpected perspectives and experiences.

The art of the pivot is not just about seizing opportunities you might not have thought of before, it's using those experiences later for your own academic, personal, or professional growth. If I had not taken a Pakistani foreign policy class, then I probably wouldn't have written my IAF 400 thesis comparing the Pakistani and Iranian nuclear programs. If I had not taken a security studies course at HKBU, I might not have taken the path that led to my master's in security policy studies. If I let the small inklings of disappointment in my Peace Corps assignment grow, I might not have fallen in love with Tanzania. I've learned that leveraging experiences allows us to take the next step after the "pivot," which is why it is important to be open to the growth potential of programs like study abroad.

Lesson 2: "That Which Harms, Also Teaches"

Just three weeks into my semester abroad in Hong Kong, I find myself walking into a tattoo parlor, ready to sit for a session to get a Latin proverb that has stuck with me for years tattooed on my arm: "*Quod nocet, saepe docet*," which loosely translates to "that which harms, also teaches." As cliché as that might be, when I find myself experiencing some of the lowest lows of any experience, I'm constantly reminded that resilience-building is a never-ending journey, and that each experience, challenge, trial, or tribulation we face offers a lesson.

Lesson 3: Trust Your Guts, but Not Your Farts

A few months into my study abroad experience in May 2012, I decided that one of the best things about my study abroad experience in Hong Kong was my class schedule. I lucked out by only having classes on Tuesdays and Wednesdays and a one-hour seminar on Thursday mornings, leaving me with a four-day weekend to explore Hong Kong. One day, I found myself on the ferry to Cheung Chau Island. Also known as Dumbbell Island, Cheung Chau is one of the more developed islands of Hong Kong and has been a traditional fishing village for many years. It has several temples and shrines and even rock carvings along with a cave where, legend has it, a pirate hid his treasure while sailing across the bay. Because of the island's size and strange shape, long trails crisscross the three main nodes of Cheung Chau.

Time passed quickly, and by mid-afternoon, despite walking around for a few hours, I realized that I hadn't visited the pirate cave yet. I looked at my phone, and then at the timetable for the ferry back, and thought to myself, "This cave can't be that far now," so I kept going.

Soon, dusk turned to darkness and I was still crossing the southern part of the island to get to the cave. As I started to descend Peak Road to get to the cave, I found myself approaching a crematorium and cemetery. I thought to myself, "This is a little spooky, maybe I should turn back," but I decided to ignore that little voice inside me and keep going. After passing the cemetery, I approached a forested area. Ignoring my intuition, I carried on, convinced that the cave was not too far ahead. As I was walking through the forest, I stepped on a large branch that snapped in half, sending out a loud echo between the trees. I stopped for a second, and in that brief moment, I heard a scurrying pitter-patter of paws running on the leaf-strewn ground.

I turned back to see a pack of five or six large dogs chasing after me. I started running, rolled onto a nearby ledge, and then ran up the hill toward the cemetery. For some reason that I still don't know to this day, the dogs stayed below the ledge and kept barking. I slowly walked across the top of the hill to safety.

What would I do differently if given the chance? As I was writing my initial study abroad blog posts, I often complained about Hong Kong, from describing how I felt like my study abroad semester was "interrupting" my college experience to my disagreements with my professors. In retrospect, I learned so much that I was able to leverage during my graduate studies in security policy studies. I wish I had gone into my semester abroad with *fewer* expectations. I've since learned keeping an open mind helps me embrace the unknown, learn from new experiences, adapt to uncertainties, and find the positive in all situations.

If you take anything from this narrative, let it be these lessons:

- Be fully open to the experience so you can get the most out of it in terms of the pivot, the silver linings in the tough times, or the growth you'll undoubtedly experience, no matter how immediate or delayed those realizations might be.

- Be prepared to ask locals questions, make mistakes, and explore, even alone, if it is safe to do so.

- Don't be afraid to ask locals for their recommendations on places to eat, things to see, or activities to do.

- Try to pick up some of the language if you can before traveling to ease this process of exploration.

A semester in Hong Kong might not have made sense to me at the time, but it does make sense now. I realize that my adaptability, resilience, and resolve—traits that have afforded me academic and professional success—were honed during my time in Hong Kong. For that, I can now say I am truly grateful for my study abroad experience.

Whether you are writing an admissions essay, applying to a graduate program, pursuing an academic or professional fellowship, or interviewing for a job after graduation, the skills you can gain from studying abroad can set you apart from other applicants. In my own job interviews in the extremely competitive international development field in Washington, DC, I have been able to cite my adaptability, resilience, and resolve drawn from the lessons I learned in Hong Kong. During these stages of any interview process, interviewers do not just want to hear *what* you have accomplished—which they can read from your resume or transcript—but *how* you achieved these goals. These experiences differentiate you from other applicants. In my interviews, I have drawn on my study abroad experience to talk about cultural competence and intercultural communications, which are essential in any office or academic setting. I have also drawn on my problem-solving skills, networking, cross-cultural collaboration and team building, independence, flexibility, and desire for self-discovery and growth. These are attributes that no resume can capture.

Who knows? Maybe one day, you will find yourself standing in Willingham Hall before an audience of young Mercerians, reflecting on your own experiences, or writing to inspire the next generation of students to put their majors in "changing the world" to good use.

7

BIRTHDAY SPAGHETTI: HOW LEARNING ABOUT GUINEA HELPED ME LEARN ABOUT MYSELF

Sarah Harris

Majors: International Affairs and French
Minor: Global Development
Class of 2020

"A day of traveling will bring a basketful of learning."
—Vietnamese Proverb

Reading about travel experiences can be inspiring, but it doesn't replace creating your own. In the summer of 2018, I participated in a Mercer on Mission trip to N'Zérékoré, Guinea. Our service project focused on teaching English and assisting with other projects at the orphanage Home of Hope, founded and operated by a Mercer graduate, Sam Johnson. My primary motivation to participate in this program was to practice my French. I jumped at any opportunity to surround myself with the language, especially if it involved communicating with native speakers.

N'Zérékoré is the second largest city in Guinea, a country on the coast of West Africa. The city hosts a sizeable refugee and immigrant population, mostly from Liberia and Sierra Leone. Because of this blended culture, there are many English speakers and a reasonable need for English language education. However, getting there took quite a journey: we had to fly into Conakry, travel by car for a full day to Kankan, spend the night, and then spend another day traveling by car until we arrived in N'Zérékoré.

After the whirlwind three-week trip with my Mercer on Mission team ended, I felt a desire to continue discovering this new environment and deepen my understanding of this new culture.. A three-month internship after the Mercer on Mission trip gave me the opportunity to continue working with Dr. Houry, Sam Johnson, and the study abroad office. During the three months, another student and I were tasked with designing and leading English classes in the orphanage, at a private high school, and a university. We continued to help with community outreach and bridge-building projects alongside the orphanage and a corresponding Christian organization, such as donating sugar to a mosque to support the celebration of Ramadan and providing rice for a refugee camp.

I wish I had been better prepared for my responsibilities in N'Zérékoré. I had never taught a real English class before, especially not at the university level, so the assignment was overwhelming. In hindsight, I should have taken steps before my trip to ask professors how to prepare for classes at these levels. I could have initiated conversations with Sam and other locals to learn what to expect from the classes. Using these insights, asking professors for guidance, and researching teaching content and strategies would have helped me feel more prepared from the beginning. Additionally, when I did feel unprepared, I would advise my past self to take advantage of the resources I had. While I spoke with the other intern and Sam Johnson, it would have been helpful to consult with professors and other teachers at the school for more support.

It may be obvious, but the French spoken in Guinea is different from the French spoken in France. Most of my classes were taught in "standard" French, and every person I had spoken to in French before my time in Guinea was either French or spoke with a standard French accent. Learning to adapt to different pronunciations and vocabulary was valuable. As a language lover, it's important to be able to diversify the source of your language learning. This also ties in with being decentered—it forces us to answer the question of what makes something "standard" and who has the power to decide international norms and why.

Speaking another language, even just a few words, was a quick way for me to establish a meaningful connection with residents. I picked up a few words in Kpelle, the local language in N'Zérékoré, and it seemed that people at the market and elsewhere appreciated that I said "hello" in their language. Even if all I could say was "hello" before switching to French, it still showed I was making an effort. This is a lesson I have applied in multiple environments. I briefly interned at a refugee resettlement agency where a lot of clients spoke Swahili, and while I only knew the basics, it was clear that greeting them in Swahili made them feel more comfortable for the rest of the interactions. Demonstrating basic language skills in the host country showed my willingness to work with them rather than forcing my cultural expectations on them.

As the three months passed, I realized how much I had yet to discover about N'Zérékoré and the country of Guinea. This feeling is one that I still carry no matter where I go. This was the case when I moved to France and when I briefly lived in Morocco. After all these experiences, I have come to realize that I love the process of seeing how much I don't understand about a place and then growing to understand it more. A major conclusion I drew from my time in Guinea that has stayed with me is how important it is to decenter myself in my interactions with N'Zérékoré residents. While I hadn't had much prior exposure to Islamic culture and customs, most Guineans are Muslim. My colleagues and I always had to make sure we were dressed appropriately when we went out into the community, and it was my first time hearing the call to prayer.

Other local traditions were completely new to me. I remember being invited to a birthday party at a club for someone I had never met before. We sat in a room that looked like a lot of clubs in the

United States, with booths and tables and room to dance. Spaghetti was served as the birthday meal, a traditional choice in Guinea. There was no cake in sight. The birthday girl had given the DJ a list of all the guests as if they would take attendance. To earn a plate of spaghetti, the DJ called upon each person to step into the middle of the floor, dance, drop off a gift at a table, toss small amounts of money at the birthday girl, and give a speech about her. I had never been to a birthday party like this before, or eaten spaghetti to celebrate someone, but who was I to say this wasn't a perfectly valid way to celebrate? In a dramatically different environment, I learned quickly that my predispositions and judgments weren't going to help me get by, so I had to let them go. When working in multicultural environments, you have to accept people for who they are and meet them where they are. In my classes back at Mercer, we studied the impacts of humanitarian organizations misusing their power in local communities, including countless failed health missions attributed to a lack of trust between humanitarian staff and the people they came to assist. Taking the time to understand others and their perspectives is a relatively small effort that goes a long way.

As I began to learn what life was like in N'Zérékoré, I gained confidence. For example, one of the main ways we traveled around the city was via "taxi moto"—motorcycle taxis whose drivers wore brightly colored vests to indicate they were accepting patrons. After a few weeks of living in Guinea, I knew it cost 5,000 Guinean francs to get from where we were staying to where I was working. So, when a driver tried to charge me 10,000, I told him, "I know it's only 5,000." He laughed and conceded, I gave him 5,000 Guinean francs, and he went on his way. Before this experience, I would never have felt comfortable speaking up for myself like that, but I knew the price and the value of the currency in a meaningful way. Learning how to live in an environment so different from what I was used to laid the foundation for all my future travels. Whenever I have lived in or visited another place, I had the confidence of knowing I could figure something out. In this way, I shifted my perspective of viewing travel as something stressful to viewing it as a puzzle I had yet to understand, but eventually would. This confidence showed itself in small ways too, like asserting myself with the taxi moto driver or bargaining at the market. These ways of communicating with others, especially people I didn't know, were previously uncomfortable to me. But since these practices were local norms, and the other option would be spending extra money due to shyness, I was pushed to adapt, which has built my confidence in the years following my time in Guinea.

Before I traveled outside the US, I didn't feel like there was much of a united American culture. But once I spent time abroad, I noticed there are certain aspects of myself that are distinctly American. When in a different country, you get more of a bird's eye view of your home country and realize there are certain similarities across the country. I developed a better sense of American identity because I had to confront it all the time. I had to explain my identity to others and question my instincts. A huge benefit of this type of confrontation was realizing there are certain elements of each country that I prefer or don't prefer, such as how success is viewed, how important the family unit is, and how the community is built. And in seeing things that look different, I was allowed to reflect on how I've seen similar situations handled before in my environment. This kind of opportunity gives a deep cultural self-consciousness.

If you are considering traveling abroad, I would highly recommend the following:

- Utilize whatever resources are available to you to better understand the country's history and anticipate what to expect before you go.
- Listen to the radio, find social media posts, and explore Wikipedia.

- If there is a relevant class, take it; if you know someone with ties or history in that country, talk to them!

Begin researching national and local customs and norms before you travel abroad. This will allow you to immediately begin exploring the deeper social context that exists in different communities. Your experience will be enriched so much more.

It isn't until we exit our bubble that we can truly critically think about the life we want to lead and the environment we want to find ourselves in. After my time in Guinea, I spent my final undergraduate spring break on a faculty-led trip to the United Arab Emirates. What made this trip different from my experience preparing for Guinea is that we took a class in the weeks leading up to the trip in which we studied and discussed the economic and political history of the country, focusing on Dubai, where we spent most of our time. Having this background made the trip so meaningful because we were able to see elements of what we had studied. Additionally, we had the chance to speak with some of the people living there, both native residents and immigrants, and made the most of this opportunity by asking pointed, thought-out questions.

Along with these wonderful aspects of exploring, the growth studying abroad elicits does come at the cost of feeling lonely sometimes, as traveling can also be isolating. This was especially the case when I was in Guinea because it wasn't uncommon for us to lose internet access which meant losing contact with our families for a few days at a time! Maybe you come to realize you miss hearing someone speak in your accent or eating a food item you don't even like when you are home. I couldn't have imagined I'd yearn to hear a Southern accent, but I felt a strange sense of comfort once I was on the flight back to Atlanta and heard a Southern drawl. All to say, it's normal to feel isolated. In some ways, loneliness is part of the process.

As a young adult preparing for a future career abroad, I now consider a wide range of job prospects and locations anywhere in the world. To be sure, I would not be confident that I could succeed in a new environment without having had previous exposure in the context of these programs.

Initially, I felt hesitant to spend a whole semester away from my friends, family, and the life I knew on campus. In hindsight, I'm grateful I took advantage of the opportunities available to me because it was eye-opening to truly understand how people in different parts of the world experience life. Studying and living abroad opens you up to new ways of thinking and being in the world. The value of the interactions you have with others who are different from you is something you simply have to travel to harness.

8

DIZZY SPELLS, D-DAY, AND DEVELOPMENT: A STORY OF PERSONAL GROWTH THROUGH STUDY ABROAD

Michael Mathews

Global Development Studies
Class of 2020

"We must never forget the explorer's spirit."
—Japanese Proverb

People who have spent most of their lives in the United States live in a fantasy. The American government's power, the nation's unparalleled financial might, and the protection provided by two oceans and two allied neighbors create an illusion that America is the world. For a long time, I had this view. Our information, news, and political discourse are often insular. We have the privilege of engaging with the world as we choose. The balance between engagement and isolationism is a constant struggle in our country.

Studying abroad burst my domestic bubble. As a global development studies (GDS) major, I chose a course of study and a career path that took me away from our familiar shores. Along with the Department of International and Global Studies' sister majors of international affairs (IA) and global health (GH), all who select such dynamic and pertinent degrees must broaden their horizons, mentally and physically. I think any major that contains the words "international" or "global" that does not require studying abroad is inadequate.

Many Americans like me have the privilege/curse that their mother tongue is the global lingua franca. It can seem that the whole world speaks English, but it does not. Studying abroad and acquiring second-language skills are invaluable for personal growth, career marketability, and becoming a well-rounded global citizen. I chose Mercer on Mission South Africa (MOMSA) for a few simple reasons. First, I knew, liked, and trusted the professors who led the trip, Dr. Houry and Dr. Morgan. Dr. Houry was the head of the Department of International and Global Studies and my academic advisor. If he was going to South Africa, and I had to study abroad as a major requirement, why would I not go on his trip? Second, the MOMSA trip is often comprised of other IA/GDS/GH majors; going abroad with my friends and classmates added a level of comfort and familiarity that I needed. A fifteen-hour flight and a month away from home could be overwhelming without a familiar and well-established learning environment. Third, MOMSA was the only study abroad program offered in a nation that spoke English as one of its national languages and did not require extra vaccinations. I detest oral pills, and the idea of having to take a daily oral malarial medication and receive additional vaccines to be a part of the Mercer on Mission Tanzania trip was excruciating. Fourth, and finally, as a student of color, I was attracted to visiting an ethnically diverse but majority-black nation with a complex and rich history like the United States. MOMSA ticked all my boxes, and I was pleased to receive a spot on the trip.

MOMSA required us to do pre-travel readings and attend weekly meetings and discussions to prepare us for our time in the country. We studied the history of South Africa's political development with a particular focus on apartheid, the defining political, cultural, and economic system of South Africa that wholly shaped the modern nation. Any students seeking to learn about this remarkable country will need an understanding of this tragic, cruel, and unnatural system to comprehend South Africa. The readings, films, and group discussions we used to prepare for the trip pushed us to examine the tangled relationship between race, class, economic status, and national unity in our own country and South Africa. The stateside preparation was a vital foundation for the subsequent in-country experiences and did a great deal to assist my cultural understanding.

As a novice traveler, I was excited to go to South Africa while also not fully processing what I had signed up. My only international experience was a pair of short cruises to the Caribbean with my family. I only got off the ship for an afternoon in the Bahamas. Still, I do not count an afternoon in the Bahamas as a real experience abroad. South Africa would be different. Spending extensive time in the country would provide a more well-rounded view of the nation than just a trip between hotels and beaches.

Our assignment with MOMSA was to work in primary schools in four different communities in Cape Town and assist the teachers and school administration in developing sustainable leadership and anti-bullying activities. Additionally, we worked with students on their public speaking skills by holding a multi-school debate on critical student issues, such as school uniforms. We focused on creating lesson plans and programs for the schools to continue to use and adapt as they saw fit. The activities had to be replicable with existing available resources at the schools. We did not want to place any additional financial burden on the schools graciously hosting us by saddling them with costly activities requiring non-local supplies.

Getting the children to go from shy to talkative to debaters took time and quite a bit of coaxing, but it was well worth the effort. With patience and some editing, we assisted the students in crafting "for" and "against" arguments for their given topics. They developed succinct and moving narratives for their opening statements and thoroughly enjoyed cross-examining each other. By the end of the debate preparation, the students were thinking quickly on their feet and able to come up with rebuttals on the fly. Their enthusiasm for debating and public speaking was a sight to see.

One of the most striking things I noticed about South Africa was the coexistence of poverty and wealth. The distribution of economic resources and opportunities is unequal in South Africa, with many of the problems stemming from apartheid. I recall seeing the shacks and townships on the side of the highway on the bus ride into Cape Town from the airport. South Africa did not attempt to hide the reality of the desperate living conditions for hundreds of thousands of its citizens. You could look away or focus on your phone, but the townships were there. Thousands of people, maybe tens of thousands, live in sheet metal homes without many of the modern conveniences people like me take for granted: reliable electricity and water, well-maintained public infrastructure, adequately funded schools, and dependable public safety. The scenery just off the plane from Johannesburg, South Africa, had already expanded my worldview.

The housing crisis in South Africa left me with another poignant experience. One morning, my group discussed similarities and differences between South Africa and the United States with a class of fifth-year students (ages ten to eleven). One of the students asked our group, "Does America have shacks?" The student was intimately familiar with South African shacks and the large townships I had seen during my first hours in the country. The question took us by surprise. We were silent momentarily and looked at each other for a moment. We eventually told her the truth. America does not have large townships like South Africa. We have people who are homeless and who do not have a regular, safe place to sleep. We have people who live in not very nice apartments and mobile homes, but not shacks. We told them that some people who are homeless live in makeshift communities underneath bridges, in abandoned buildings, and in wooded areas of large cities, but once again, these were not shacks, nor were they townships. The kids knew that not everyone in America lived in a big house like they saw on TV or in movies. Throughout the classroom, we saw a mix of disappointment and happiness in response to these answers. For some students, it was a relief to learn that America was not dealing with the permanence of townships and the long-term inability to build and provide traditional housing accommodations for such a large number of people. Other children were uneasy learning about another stark economic and societal difference between South Africa and America.

As students studying abroad, we felt woefully unprepared and unqualified to answer such a question. We were college students living cushy lives about to spend a summer in South Africa. None of us were unhoused or lived in poor housing conditions. The discussion we had afterward was frank and reflective. We came to South Africa to learn about their country and grappled with one of our nation's persistent hush-hush problems. That insightful and earnest question from a fifth-year student has lingered since then. South Africa helped me and my classmates become better global and US citizens. We returned to Atlanta with various positive and negative insights and an empathetic understanding of other people's journeys, which helped us become more compassionate students and community members.

Studying abroad is rewarding, exhilarating, scary, and life-changing. While in Cape Town, I explored and learned about a stunningly beautiful world city with thousands of years of history. The natural beauty of Table Mountain, towering more than 3,563 feet high (1,086 meters) and overlooking the Cape, is well worth a long plane ride. Looking out for tens of miles over the city below and the endless ocean in front gave me a sense of perspective that is difficult to come by at sea level. I took one of my most treasured photographs with one of my closest friends at Table Mountain. It is a photo that has continued to connect us despite life leading us to live two continents apart.

MOMSA was not all southern sunshine and trips to vineyards in Stellenbosch. About three weeks into the trip, I caught a cold. I was the fourth or fifth student to have the sniffles since we arrived in the country; working with school children is not without risks. However, unlike the others, who quickly recovered, I did not. My cold became an inner ear infection that affected my coordination and balance. After a few days of severe balance issues, I had to go to a local hospital for an examination by a doctor. I was diagnosed with vertigo and told to limit my activities and movement for the rest of the trip. I could not do many of the final-week excursions with my classmates. Thankfully, not only were the professors , but so were the hosts of our guest house. Someone routinely checked in on me and ensured I was doing okay.

Outside of our work in South Africa, my classmates included me in as many activities as possible. They brought back treats and snacks from excursions and kept me well stocked with gifts to bring back to my friends and family at home. Finally, they convinced me to be brave and at least attend the safari park tour. No walking was involved. I could sit in an open-air jeep and look at the animals; motor vehicle travel was one of the few things that caused my vertigo to abate. A bit of peer pressure and two hours later, I was having a fantastic time seeing the "big five" African land animals—lion, leopard, elephant, rhinoceros, and African buffalo—roam with freedom of movement. My classmates made the trip a 10/10 experience despite the vertigo because of their kindness, generosity, and patience. Bears do stick together. Little did I know that my South African medical hiccup was only the beginning of the defining struggles of my college years: a two-year-long ordeal with vertigo and my love/hate relationship with French language classes.

The return to Mercer in the spring of 2017 after my medical withdrawal was painful, slow, and isolating. Unlike the previous year, I was not living with my friends. I was adjusting to being back in school full time but was still not fully back to who I was. I struggled with daily aspects of life, and walking was still not easy for me. I had to take breaks during my walk from my loft at Mercer Village to Knight Hall. I was constantly worried that my balance would fail and I would fall. I was anxious, and I could only cope with going home each weekend to rest and recharge for the upcoming week. My parents worked miracles for me, picking me up each Friday night and dropping me off again Sunday afternoon.

My course load that year also proved daunting. After taking years of Spanish in grade school, I decided to expand my language skills by pursuing French classes to complete the language requirement of my global development studies major. While I managed to scrape along in my introductory French course, French 112 proved to be my most challenging course at Mercer. We progressed rapidly, and I quickly fell behind. I had to work with the professor outside of class and receive extra help to catch up.

I was struggling because I had not entirely accepted French internally. I was still trying to think in English and then translate to French. I had to move past that to create space for a French way of thinking and understanding. That took more time, and I could only truly internalize the language when I began incorporating French into my personal life. I watched Netflix with French subtitles, found French-language YouTube history channels, and changed my FIFA 2017 settings to put my commentary language in French. All of these steps helped me to improve my language skills, which proved fruitful for the remaining two years at Mercer. I chose to minor in French, which required taking two classes in the language each semester, and although I took daily classes in French, I was never an A student. I celebrated Bs but mostly earned hard-fought Cs. I grew to love the language and, later, the people.

I jumped at the chance to put my language skills to real-world use by going to Normandy, France, for spring break 2019. Usually, spring break trips involve beaches; ours did too, just not warm ones. Instead, our beaches were cold, windswept, and pocketed with the remnants of seventy-five-year-old shell craters. Rather than Daytona, Cocoa, or West Palm, these beaches were called Omaha, Utah, Sword, Gold, and Juno. This trip was in conjunction with Mercer Army ROTC, which had been visiting Normandy for years as a part of a culminating project for the cadets. Spring 2019 was the first year ROTC brought along some French "experts" to for translation.

We prepared for Normandy by watching *Band of Brothers* with the cadets and army captain who led our trip, Capt. Walt. We studied the battle plans of Operation Overlord, the code name for the Allies' invasion and liberation of Normandy. Capt. Walt, a WWII history buff, brought his collection of airborne equipment. We held the weapons the soldiers used during their battles, like the M1 Garand. The soldiers were the same age as we were, yet they would have dropped into a warzone with seventy pounds of gear instead of examining it as memorabilia. I was allowed to keep one of the French guidebooks the American soldiers were told to use once they reached the ground and found their bearings. Thankfully, I knew more than they did about French if I ever got lost.

We stayed in Bayeux, France, a small city in Normandy known for the Bayeux Tapestry, an embroidered cloth that details the Norman invasion of England, led by William the Conqueror. We had the opportunity to see it and had many other incredible experiences. We visited the Normandy beaches and the American cemeteries; seeing where such a monumental historical event had occurred was unforgettable. Another memorable excursion was the D-Day experience near Carrefour, the name of the vital crossroads the Allies had to capture to secure the beach landing zones and push deeper into the Norman interior. This museum and ride allowed guests to participate in a recreation of D-Day, from receiving orders to gearing up and departing England to drop behind the German lines. I did not grasp that our plane was one of the many unlucky ones that did not complete their mission. We were shot down by German antiaircraft fire. The whole group laughed as I said far too loudly, "Damn, guys, I didn't know we were dead!" I would not have been on that trip without growing to love French. Three required semesters of French coursework may also take you to France. I am all the better for it.

MOMSA also taught me a lesson on migration, assimilation, and integration. While working in the primary schools, I spent one morning sitting with a child who had recently arrived from Zimbabwe. We sat and talked for two hours after I had chased him down to stop him from leaving school early that day by passing through a gap in the exterior fence. This troubled child said he felt isolated and unseen in South Africa. He was of a different ethnic background than most of the students in the school. He did not speak Afrikaans, nor was he confident in English yet. Afrikaans was the native language of many schoolchildren, with English being the national language of education in South Africa. For a ten-year-old to deal with such severe challenges integrating into a new country, culture, and language was beyond what I had experienced in my own life. I do not know if the child grew to adapt to life in South Africa with time, but I hope he did. MOMSA and France allowed me to start seeing the world outside my native lens.

Reflecting on issues abroad expanded my understanding of issues at home. I developed a more compassionate view of immigration and migration that continues to evolve today. The dangers of moving across borders are immense. The goal of a good life is the far end of a dark tunnel with obstacles, traps, and setbacks for the tens of millions of people who have been forced, for economic, political, religious, or security reasons, to leave their home country and build a life elsewhere.

In 2022, after failing a routine hearing test before beginning a job, I learned that the cause of all the trouble in South Africa was not a cold. I have otosclerosis, a condition that leads to abnormal bone growth in the middle ear. It causes hearing loss as well as balance issues. What began in Cape Town as a cold was an underlying medical condition that would have occurred anywhere. Otosclerosis usually shows itself in one's early twenties, and I was exactly twenty years old in South Africa. All the ups and downs that came with my experience of this medical condition would have been more upsetting and difficult if I hadn't participated in Mercer on Mission. The ordeal showed me I had a resilience I had not previously known I possessed. Things in your life can go wrong unexpectedly, but you can adapt.

Not only adapt, but later thrive. What once held me back and deprived me of six months of learning and growing with my friends has now transformed me. It has given me an appreciation for the hidden struggles and conditions many suffer silently. I wear a hearing aid in my left ear; it's small and discreet, a stealthy upgrade. If anyone happens to see it, which is not easy, it resembles a standard earbud. My quality of life has improved since I started wearing it. It makes for a funny story: the man in his twenties getting a hearing aid with eighty-year-olds. I have since noticed and met many people who have hearing aids and other sound-amplifying devices, a trend I was unaware of before my own experience. I would not change a thing about my journey to a diagnosis or where it all began, at a guesthouse in Pinelands, Cape Town, South Africa.

In a life-changing way, study abroad shaped my current trajectory. I would not have had the opportunity to work and live outside the United States without the prior experience. It was necessary from a resume-building aspect and, more importantly, a character-building experience. The good, the bad, the uncomfortable, the joyous, and everything that happened to me from 2020 to 2021 was built on the foundation of a successful study abroad.

Studying abroad has bolstered my future career path, which I hope will lead to work inside the federal government.

Before you decide to study abroad, begin the process of self-examination. *Why are you choosing to do this specific trip? What are you hoping to gain from this experience?* Reflection on these questions and more is the basis for a successful and possibly transformative study abroad experience. Be realistic in what you hope to do, see, and understand. The main point of such trips is to learn and grow. *How do you plan to do this? What are your fears? What are you worried about going wrong?* International travel is not without risk; be open and honest with yourself and your support system about your concerns. They may be unfounded, and they may not. To have reservations is natural; do not ignore these feelings but explore them actively. You may be able to overcome these worries or doubts or learn to live with them as you travel.

Embrace the unexpected and savor the perfect moments of life. You may not know it until after the fact, but you will be better for it once you realize it. The challenges and obstacles that lie ahead may be substantial. They may require not only a diversion of your time and energy but a total commitment until you have settled them. The difficulties may not end after six months or a year; instead, they may linger with you. That's okay. The bad can shape us just as much as the good. Hearing loss and vertigo did not keep me down for good, just for a bit of time. I had to find my courage and allow others to help me along the way. My family, friends, professors, and classmates have been my greatest assets; without them, the measured level of success I have achieved would have been impossible. I hope they understand just how thankful and appreciative I am for them.

Good luck on your travels, my fellow Mercerians!

LIFESTYLE CHANGE

9

BECOMING A GLOBAL CITIZEN: THE TRANSFORMATIVE POWER OF STUDY ABROAD

Bryant E. Harden

Political Science
Class of 2011

"Little by little, one travels far."
—Spanish Proverb

One of my most vivid memories is on a bus in South Africa. For many in the study abroad program, this was our first experience outside of the United States, and we were excited to *see* Cape Town. As we exited the airport, we enthusiastically pointed out the terrain and the messages welcoming travelers who were arriving for the World Cup. After twenty minutes on the bus, the lively banter had gone silent. As we moved away from the airport, the Coca-Cola signs for the World Cup were few and far between. Instead, we saw the signs of apartheid—the tires being burned for warmth, the shelters made from scrap materials, and the power lines going in all directions. The divided society that I had read about just weeks prior was right in front of me.

The journey to South Africa with my peers from Mercer University transitioned from a simple academic requirement for my political science degree to a pivotal educational experience. This transformation was fostered by my interactions with the students at Hector Peterson High School. Over the first week, our surface-level interactions eventually developed into strong personal bonds. During an exercise known as the "hot seat," we gathered around in a circle with a single chair placed in the center. With the center chair empty, the students sang traditional Xhosa songs in unison. Unexpectedly, one of the girls with whom I had made a distinct connection broke out in tears and moved to the center of the circle. While the singing continued, she shared her personal story of tragedy in which she was sexually assaulted. This act of vulnerability and cathartic release was not unique to her—one after another, students entered the circle to divulge their own stories of heartbreak. Following each testimony, the group would stand in an act of solidarity, singing songs that seemed to provide a sense of solace and communal healing.

My experiences in South Africa were pivotal and precipitated a fundamental transformation in my worldview. This change was comprehensive, altering not only my academic pursuits but also my long-term professional aspirations. My experiences culminated in a commitment to the principles and responsibilities of global citizenship. Indeed, the day I returned to the United States from South Africa, I began my application to serve as a Peace Corps volunteer. Instead of pursuing a career in US politics, this grassroots study abroad program, led by Dr. Eimad Houry and Dr. Mary Alice Morgan, empowered me to see the international as personal and engage the world as both a global citizen and professor. Such profound change underscores the inherent value and transformative potential of study abroad experiences.

The Transformative Power of Study Abroad

For me, studying abroad was more than just a geographical shift; it was a profound journey of self-discovery and growth. As I traversed unfamiliar terrains in South Africa, the United Arab Emirates, and beyond, I not only gain knowledge about the world but also glean insights into my inner self. This transformative power emerges from my deep dive into diverse cultures and the reflective spaces that these experiences carved within me. The two pivotal axes of this development are the immersion into a host culture and the introspection that it invites.

Cultural Immersion

The transformative power of study abroad stems from cultural immersion. Rather than the cursory experiences of a tourist or snapshot understanding from a textbook, my experiences studying abroad converted street corners into classrooms and meals into lessons. In this way, my unplanned conversations with South Africans were akin to class discussions. These interactions were more than just exchanges; they were insights into the history and culture of their community.

The daily life in South Africa, rich with tradition and brimming with change, provided an authentic lens through which to view the region's social fabric. To truly engage with that culture, I had to step beyond the role of an observer and leap into active participation. It is through involvement in local practices, an appreciation for the community's societal norms, and attendance at cultural events that a deeper, more meaningful transformation occurs. This level of engagement fosters an understanding of the intricacies of a society, encompassing both its storied past and its evolving present.

Indeed, this sort of cultural immersion created a space for me to *feel* with all of my senses the challenges and triumphs of a society, which in turn fostered empathy and a nuanced perspective that textbooks had not provided. The streets of South Africa, lined with the narratives of its people, the struggle for equality, and the celebration of postapartheid progress, offered an unparalleled education in the resilience and diversity of the human spirit. It is within this context that the nuances of society emerge, not just as observed phenomena but as lived experiences. This comprehensive involvement is what transforms a foreign environment from a place of study to a place of profound personal growth and insight, ultimately shaping myself and others into informed global citizens equipped to contribute meaningfully to the global community.

Forced Self-Reflection

Studying abroad requires a reckoning with the similarities and differences between cultures and, as such, serves as an external catalyst for self-reflection. The faces, tales, and surroundings create moments of epiphany, which shape personal beliefs, attitudes, and visions for the future. In this way, studying abroad positions the world as a mirror to those beliefs and behaviors that have otherwise been understood as *normal* and comfortable.

In South Africa, each shared story, panoramic view, or fleeting moment provoked reflection. Amidst the vibrant culture, I found moments of introspection, juxtaposing my life with the narratives I encountered. I am reminded of Martin Luther King Jr.'s (1963) description of the power of nonviolent direct action: "Just as Socrates felt that it was necessary to create a tension in the mind so that individuals could rise from the bondage of myths and half-truths to the unfettered realm of creative analysis and objective appraisal, so must we see the need for nonviolent gadflies to create the kind of tension in society that will help men rise from the dark depths of prejudice and racism to the majestic heights of understanding and brotherhood." It is the direct proximity to cultures that are dissimilar to our own that invites us to reflect on the "truths" that we have been exposed to about others. Culture shock thus serves as an invitation and a catalyst for us to engage our world—to become global citizens.

Making the Most of Your Experiences

To truly harness the power of studying abroad, one must approach it with intentionality and an openness to adapt and learn. It is not merely about being physically present in a different location; rather it is about immersing oneself mentally and emotionally. Navigating this path requires a balanced mix of receptiveness to new information and proactively seeking enriching interactions. Two strategies elevated my study abroad experiences from merely informative to truly transformative: first, adopting the mindset of a blank canvas, devoid of biases, and ready to absorb fresh perspectives; and second, forging genuine friendships that offer deeper insights into local customs, values, and worldviews.

Embracing the Blank Canvas

Approaching my international experiences with the mindset of a blank canvas is akin to opening a book without preconceived notions of its contents. It involves shedding stereotypes and biases, allowing the culture and environment to shape my understanding organically. This approach has encouraged me to resist the temptation of relying solely on preconceived ideas about a country that I am visiting. This advice first resonated with me as I prepared to depart for Mongolia with the Peace Corps. Although others and I were eager to read as much as we could about Mongolia and start learning the language, the volunteers who were then serving in Mongolia suggested otherwise: put down the books and consider arriving with an open mind. They stressed the value of learning on the ground and engaging with the community without imposing preconceived ideas.

Importantly, keeping a blank canvas mindset does not mean ignoring the historical and cultural context of your destination. Instead, it encourages us to view those contexts as general starting points, allowing the nuances of daily life and personal interactions to color the canvas. By approaching my international experiences in this way, I not only gain a richer understanding of the host culture but I also participate in breaking down stereotypes and fostering genuine connections.

Engaging Our World

Another important lesson is that studying abroad is not a passive experience; rather, it is an opportunity to actively engage with the world around you. Embracing this mindset involves seizing every opportunity to immerse yourself in local activities, events, and social gatherings. When I receive an invitation to a cultural celebration, a community event, or a local gathering, I say yes. This proactive engagement has not only enriched my experiences but has also opened doors to some of my most meaningful connections and insights.

Being an active participant in the host community allows us to go beyond the surface level of cultural understanding. Whether it's joining a sports club, volunteering for a local cause, or participating in language exchange programs, these activities provide avenues to connect with people on a deeper level. By embracing opportunities to step out of our comfort zone and participate in the vibrant tapestry of the host culture, we not only enrich ourselves but also contribute positively to the community that we temporarily call home.

Conclusion

Reflecting on my journey from that transformative bus ride in South Africa to my profound engagements in Mongolia, Dubai, and beyond, my experiences abroad coalesce into a narrative of growth, self-discovery, and global citizenship. The initial shock of witnessing the stark realities of apartheid set the stage for a series of meaningful connections and cultural immersions that expanded my worldview. For me, the transformative power of studying abroad lies in the synergy between cultural immersion and forced self-reflection. As I continue to navigate unfamiliar terrains, I seek to embrace the mindset of a blank canvas and actively engage with the world around me to foster genuine connections. These experiences collectively underscore the value of intentional, immersive experiences that not only inform but truly transform.

While this chapter has detailed the transformative power of studying abroad in my life, it is equally important to recognize the people who support and mentor us, not just during our time abroad but long after. Their dedication and investment behind the scenes are what truly shape these life-changing experiences. For me, that person is Eimad Houry. My journey started with him co-leading my first international experience in South Africa, but his impact did not end there. Dr. Houry became a constant presence, discussing research projects during my Peace Corps service in Mongolia, advising on master's programs in the United Kingdom, inviting me to co-lead study abroad programs in Dubai, mentoring me as I entered the classroom to teach international affairs at Mercer, supporting my doctoral studies at the University of Florida, acting as a sounding board as I developed a Mercer On Mission program to Mongolia, and supporting my decision to teach and direct the Global Citizenship Certificate program at Florida State University. Dr. Houry's impact on my life's trajectory cannot be understated, and I will be forever grateful for his mentorship and the transformative experiences that he has led over the years.

10

IS EATING FRUIT AFTER A MEAL BETTER FOR DIGESTION? ENGAGING NEW WAYS OF LIVING AS A WORLD TRAVELER

Anna Cizek

International Affairs, Global Health, French
Class of 2017

"Wisdom can be found traveling."
—Sri Lankan Proverb

My first opportunity to travel outside of the United States was when I was a sophomore at Mercer University. As a prospective student, I learned that Mercer had a program called Mercer on Mission that provided students with service-learning opportunities abroad. At first, I was concerned that I would not be able to afford to participate in the study abroad program. However, I learned that the price of the trip was the equivalent of six credit hours, or two full-time courses. Fortunately, I was attending Mercer on a softball scholarship, so I started asking around the athletic department to see if my scholarship could be applied. I learned that if I submitted the appropriate paperwork and was approved, my scholarship could be applied to courses taken during the summer term—up to six credit hours. I was ecstatic that I had found a solution to finance my study abroad and participate in Mercer on Mission Greece!

Greece

Excited about the opportunity to study and volunteer in Greece, I completed my application materials, submitted my request to the athletic department, and conducted my interviews with the sponsoring professors. I anxiously anticipated the opportunity to participate as part of Mercer on Mission Greece's 2015 cohort. My application was denied: I did not make the cut. At this time, I learned an essential life lesson. I learned the importance of perseverance. I respected the decision of the faculty to decline my application. As an athlete, I was receptive to coaching and feedback and continuously strived to improve myself in all aspects of my life—not only as an athlete but also as a student and applicant. As a result, I reached out to the faculty and asked for feedback on how I could improve myself and strengthen my application for the next Mercer on Mission Greece opportunity in 2017.

To my surprise, in response to my follow-up inquiry, the professors sponsoring Mercer on Mission Greece reviewed my application materials again, engaged in internal discussion, and decided to take a chance on me. I was allowed to participate in Mercer on Mission Greece in 2015. One of the greatest lessons I learned at twenty years old was the value of seeking feedback in the face of failure, relentlessly persevering toward my goals, and finding ways to create opportunities for myself despite the circumstances.

In Greece, I studied archaeology, including the design of ancient temples and the attributes of Ionic and Doric columns. I have been compelled to analyze every column I come across ever since to evaluate if it contains Ionic or Doric features. I also had the opportunity to meet Mina, Nicoletta, and Vincelle, siblings living in an impoverished Roma village. Nicoletta drew me a picture, which remains on my wall to this day. I've kept it as both a memory and a reminder.

South Africa

After my service learning trip in Greece, it was evident that my understanding of international affairs was limited, and my knowledge gaps were significant. Fortunately for me, Mercer faculty recognized the need for academic programs that uprooted students from their immediate environment and pulled them out of their physical and intellectual comfort zones. In 2016, I took my first trip to the continent of Africa. I was accepted to the Mercer on Mission South Africa program, where I volunteered at Pelican Park Primary School by day and studied the history of apartheid by night. I learned that there are eleven official languages spoken in South Africa. I hiked Table Mountain and got lost. I saw penguins, I ate ostrich, and I wore a hijab.

It was my first time wearing a hijab. I would not have known how to put it on, but my primary school students knew. Coming from a predominantly Islamic community, our students were eager to show us how to wear hijabs! I was posted at Pelican Park to teach the primary school students, yet time and time again I found that I was the one learning. I did not know it at the time, but learning how to properly wear a hijab would prove very useful later on when I traveled to Islamic countries around the world and visited mosques. After my time in South Africa, I traveled to Qatar to present my undergraduate research and spent the last semester of my senior year studying abroad in Ifrane, Morocco.

France

After graduating from Mercer University, I decided to spend a year teaching English in France. I was paired with an Italian roommate, Santina, who was similarly teaching Italian in France. We lived in a town called Thionville between the French cities of Nancy and Metz. Thionville is a twenty-minute train ride from Luxembourg, which provided ample opportunity for me to travel around Europe.

I made it my mission to travel to as many countries in Europe as possible.

My roommate, Santina, thought I was crazy, but I could occasionally convince her to come with me. I discovered overnight buses and managed to travel to more than twenty countries that year. I traveled alone, I traveled with friends, and I met friends along the way.

Traveling alone was intimidating at first, but it taught me to feel comfortable being on my own. I had time to think and reflect on what was truly important to me when nobody else was there to voice their opinion. I learned how to make my own decisions, be my leader, and solve my problems.

During my time in France, I lived in a high school called Lycée Charlemagne, where I taught most of my courses. The commute to work was ideal—a couple of flights of stairs! The building was also historically unique, as it was used during World War II to house US soldiers and had bullet holes to remind you of its past. Yet the environment did have its challenges. The high school did not have internet, so I learned how to live for a year without it and tried to see the lack of access, and ensuing boredom, as an opportunity for me to prioritize French language learning. While I could not go online, I could watch movies on DVD. I soon discovered a *médiathèque*, a sort of library with movies and music, a couple of blocks from Lycée Charlemagne. I would rent stacks of movies from the *médiathèque* and watch them at night on my laptop—internet-less entertainment! The constant exposure to French rapidly improved my language skills, and I scored well on the DALF French fluency exam the following year. Working and studying abroad was challenging and intimidating at times, but it ultimately provided me with the most extraordinary adventures, lessons, and memories.

Morocco

After my year in France, I returned to Morocco, this time on a Fulbright grant. I taught business courses at Ibn Zohr University in the southern city of Agadir. While I was in Agadir, I studied Arabic, French, Spanish, and Tachelhit, a Berber language spoken in southwestern Morocco. I also had the opportunity to volunteer for a local nongovernmental organization called Dar Si Hmad, where I wrote grants and mentored local students. I am often asked, "What made you so interested in the Middle East and North African region?" To which I always respond, "Dr. Houry." Dr. Houry has opened more doors for me than he will ever realize. He encouraged me to study abroad, intern with international organizations, study languages, participate in Model Arab League, and pursue my graduate degree. Dr. Houry worked with me over a weekend to complete my World Congress on Undergraduate Research application to present my research in Qatar and helped me secure the funding I needed to attend. It is also as a direct result of his mentorship and network that I was offered my first job in the cybersecurity field working as a cyber threat intelligence analyst. Dr. Houry has been an instrumental mentor and teacher in my life.

However, what Dr. Houry might not realize is the impact that he has had far beyond the scope of his classroom. Ayoub, Intissar, and Imane are examples of three Moroccan students who never had the pleasure of working with Dr. Houry but are direct beneficiaries of his academic programs. Dr. Houry spearheaded Mercer University's Model Arab League club, where he taught students Middle Eastern politics and parliamentary procedure. He chaperoned students to conferences around the United States, promoting public speaking, debate, and resolution writing. Dr. Houry also wrote letters of recommendation for me and my peers to intern and work for the Model Arab League's sponsoring organization, the National Council on US-Arab Relations. I was one of the fortunate students who participated in the Model Arab League and the National

Council on US-Arab Relations summer internship program. Inspired by Dr. Houry's mentorship, I began a Model Arab League club in Agadir, Morocco.

During my Fulbright year, the Université Internationale de Rabat hosted a Model Arab League conference. I was inspired to expose my students to some of the opportunities that I had during my undergraduate studies, including the Model Arab League. At the time, I could afford to take three students to Rabat, so I brought Ayoub, Intissar, and Imane to their first international Model Arab League conference with students from around the world. I never told them that I paid out of pocket for their transportation, lodging, and conference fees—they would not have accepted it if they knew. I just wanted them to have at least one of the many opportunities that I had access to throughout my academic career. I learned that sometimes even the smallest of efforts can have a drastic positive impact on someone's life. It was a surreal moment when I learned that things had come full circle for my student Ayoub.

After working with Fulbrighters and meeting other American students at the conference, Ayoub applied for and was awarded a Fulbright grant to study in the United States. His collaboration with an international cohort of students and his dedication to the Model Arab League contributed to his being awarded a Fulbright grant. Ayoub took advantage of these opportunities and proceeded to move to the United States to continue his studies and to participate in public speaking events. Dr. Houry's study abroad and mentorship programs have had a positive impact on students spanning around the world—even students he has never met.

Today

My worldview and perspective has been forever changed by my time living abroad. Studying abroad allowed me to create friendships around the world. Recently, I spent three weeks in a remote town in Sicily called Bisacquino. Santina, my Italian roommate from France, invited me to stay with her and her husband, Daniele, and meet their new baby, Giada.

I have been very fortunate in my experiences studying and working abroad. I have had glimpses into the lives of many people from around the world, for which I am extraordinarily grateful. Friends have invited me into their homes to share meals in Morocco, Qatar, Germany, Italy, France, Greece, and South Africa. However, I do find myself questioning things a lot more.

Why do I live the way that I live and do the things that I do? Why do I eat fruit before my meal when my Italian friends insist that fruit should be eaten after a meal? Is eating fruit after a meal better for digestion? Why does American culture prioritize timeliness at the expense of greeting one's elderly neighbor? What values should be the most important? How should I live my life?

After spending a notable amount of time studying and working abroad, I do not have the answers.

Studying abroad taught me that what I am accustomed to is not the only way of living and not necessarily the best way of living.

Regardless of the amount of time I spend abroad, or the number of countries I travel to, I will never have all the answers. However, studying abroad taught me the most important thing, which is that I need to ask questions. Whenever I find a paradox between the way I live and the way others live, I need to start digging deeper. Studying abroad taught me to reflect, think deeply, and ask questions.

Tips and Strategies to Maximize the Impact of Study Abroad

- Study the local language(s). This will expand your opportunities to have conversations with locals and learn from them. You will impress people and get better prices when bargaining! It will provide you with an additional layer of safety when navigating life abroad.

- Carry around a small notebook and jot down new words and phrases as you come across them on street signs, menus, and through conversations. Dedicate time at the end of each day or week to look up the new vocabulary
- Familiarize yourself with the local culture and participate in holidays and celebrations. Invest time in developing and sustaining relationships with the friends you meet abroad.
- If possible, stay for an extended period—months, or even a full year.
- A longer duration of time will allow you to become more fully immersed in the local culture.

11

I FELT A DESIRE FORMING: FINDING HOME AND PURPOSE EVERYWHERE I TRAVELED

Hoor Qureshi

Global Development Studies and Global Health Studies
Class of 2020

"Only one who wanders finds new paths."
—Norwegian Proverb

On September 11, 2000, my family immigrated to the United States from Pakistan. At the tender age of three years old, the world of communal living, wearing shalwar kameez and kurtas, and stopping everything for an afternoon cup of chai came to a halt. My life in the US turned into isolation from those who shared the same identity as me, wearing jeans and t-shirts, and endless sightings of fast food restaurants. We moved to a small town in North Georgia. Even at that young age, I could tell nobody in our new community looked like me, causing a sense of "otherness" that I never reconciled until my first trip abroad.

When we immigrated, I only spoke Urdu. A year later, on September 11, 2001, our nation was hit by a series of terrorist attacks that to this day we remember in the very fabric of who we are, and my parents decided English was the only language I should speak. This was a tactic born out of fear and protection—an experience and story not unique to my family, but representative of many immigrant families. At the time, I did not understand the weight of losing my mother tongue, nor did my parents. Eventually, we created a small community of our own with other immigrant Pakistani families, but I watched as they traveled home to Pakistan. My family couldn't afford to take trips like this, so for my entire childhood, my known world was not diverse in people, thinking, and culture.

I carried these feelings for years, and unbeknownst to me when I stepped foot onto Mercer University's campus in August 2015, I would embark on a journey of going abroad multiple times. I enrolled in global health and development classes that made me want to take my coursework abroad and see firsthand what I learned in the classroom. My family was finally able to go to Pakistan in December of 2016, and that changed the trajectory of everything for me. Up to that point, I only dreamed of traveling, and it was poetic justice that my first international trip since the age of three was back to the very country I moved from.

Pakistan

Although this was not a study abroad trip, it was extremely formative in shaping my desire to expand my studies internationally. While in Pakistan, I visited family, traveled to historical spots, saw the most beautiful mosques, and ate delicious, traditional food. I remember my dad, who was born and raised in Pakistan, being shocked that I assimilated so well since I couldn't fluently speak the language anymore, had never experienced things like load-shedding (rationing electricity) or been in a car on the opposite side of the road. It was very much the contrary—I found all of the differences fascinating.

Growing up in Georgia, especially in a small town, I had never experienced the sense of belonging that I felt in Pakistan. Moreover, just by being in Pakistan and around native Urdu speakers, I was remembering and using words in Urdu that I didn't even know I knew. That experience captures one incredible aspect of being abroad and taking the time to listen, see, and experience everything around you. It was almost instantaneous that when I returned to Mercer, I knew I had to find ways to study abroad because I had learned so much about my people, culture, and traditions by being on the ground and experiencing it for myself.

Japan

In 2017, Mercer was selected by the Japanese government's Kakehashi Project to send twenty-three students to Japan for an experiential spring break for eight days with a full scholarship. *Kakehashi* means "bridge" in Japanese, and the goal of the program was to foster stronger diplomatic, social, and economic relationships between Japan and the US. After we were selected, I learned that Georgia is Japan's largest trading partner in the US and Japan is one of the top foreign investors in the state. To be sure, there were immense job and networking opportunities that could come out of participating in a program like this.

Upon landing in Tokyo, Japan, our program host and translator greeted us. In Tokyo, most of our meals were hotpot-style, where I cooked alongside my classmates and we left our shoes outside of the eating area and sat cross-legged. This was how I ate a lot of my meals growing up, so it felt familiar.

The activity I most vividly remember is touring the Hiroshima Peace Memorial Museum and hearing from a survivor of the 1945 nuclear bombing. The museum featured a simulation that showed the radius of destruction caused by the bomb, a visual that was surreal to see. The survivor, whose sister was never found after the bombing, told us that the community came together and rebuilt the city quickly following the bombing, not knowing the effects of nuclear radiation. At eighty years old, she told us she had more tumors in her life than she could count, but also that she was grateful that she had lived a full life and was able to share her story with us.

Even though we were only there for eight days, there was a lot packed into our trip, including visits to two cities, Tokyo and Hiroshima, seeing historical sites, participating in cultural activities, visiting government offices, learning about the Japanese economy, networking with community and business leaders, and participating in traditional Japanese family life. This experience is one I will never forget, and I am immensely grateful to the Japanese government for inviting us to engage their culture.

South Africa

One of Mercer's flagship programs is Mercer on Mission (MOM). However, this study abroad trip was a different one than I intended in the summer of 2018. In the spring of that year, I was awarded a critical language scholarship to study Urdu in Lucknow, India. However, I was unable to accept the award after I was denied a visa to India for no imaginable reason other than my Pakistani heritage. As devastated as I was at the time, my professors at Mercer worked with me to develop an alternative summer plan. Instead, I enrolled in a MOM trip to South Africa. Unbeknownst to me at the time, this "backup plan" would change the course of my life, allowing me to continue to cultivate my passion for experiencing the world and traveling abroad.

This five-week-long MOM program consisted of two weeks of intensive coursework on Mercer's campus in Macon and three weeks of service learning in township schools located near Cape Town, South Africa. I was drawn to the South Africa MOM program due to its educational focus and because I would learn more about Islam in South Africa; I was there during the month of Ramadan and fasted from sunrise to sundown. Within Islam there is a concept called *ummah*, or community, which creates unity between Muslims around the world. Even though Islam is a minority religion in South Africa, I was intrigued to learn about the different ways in which *ummah* has allowed Islam to coexist with other religions.

I worked in Mitchell's Plain, a predominantly Coloured township with a sizable Muslim population, at Pelican Park Primary School (PPPS), and many of the female Muslim students stayed inside with me during their lunch and recess break, sharing the challenges of fasting during the month of Ramadan while attending school. When they learned that I was also Muslim, they asked me a range of questions from how I practice to whether Islam is similar or different in America. Through these conversations, we fostered a stronger connection than I anticipated.

There were many challenges and hard moments in South Africa, largely due to its complex history. I remember one of the teachers I worked with named Ms. Goolam saying, "I feel as if I am failing to teach my students," as she explained the daily challenges of teaching fifty students of varying literacy levels in one classroom. As I got to know Ms. Goolam, she told me that for seventeen years she had taught Zulu-speaking students in Durban, KwaZulu-Natal. However, now at PPPS, she had to adjust to teaching a diverse group of students who spoke a mix of English, Xhosa, and Afrikaans. In a country with eleven official languages and a wide range of ethnic groups, the day-to-day challenges of instructing in English become a harder feat to accomplish.

Although apartheid in South Africa ended almost thirty years ago, traces of the system remain, adversely affecting those in townships. Alongside my fellow MOM participants, I taught my students by fostering inclusivity, while also embracing differences, to develop a welcoming environment to learn English. Seeing the parallels between South Africa and the US, especially in the continued fight to better race relations and reduce inequalities in both nations, I felt a desire forming to continue working with vulnerable groups—racial minorities, women, and children—notably through education.

United Arab Emirates

During the spring semester of my senior year, I traveled to the United Arab Emirates (UAE) with ten other students and two faculty members for one last study abroad trip during my time at Mercer. This "experiential spring break" came at a time when I was waiting to hear decisions on postgraduate plans, having submitted applications for opportunities with Fulbright, Peace Corps, and AmeriCorps. Though it was a busy time with finals approaching, I remember thinking this trip would be the perfect way to round out my study abroad journeys.

Exploring Dubai felt like being in the Guinness World Record book in real life. I went to the world's largest indoor amusement park (owned by Warner Brothers Studios), rode the world's fastest roller coaster (owned by Ferrari), viewed the city from the world's largest frame, and, of course, visited the world's largest building, known as the Burj Khalifa. We went during sunset and it was one of the most beautiful experiences I've had.

Another unique thing about the UAE is the profound sense of traditionalism juxtaposed with modernism. Beyond the skyscrapers, it has both the desert terrain associated with many countries in the Middle East and a peninsula that makes for some beautiful scenery. On this trip, we had excursions where we rode through dunes, rode camels, held eagles in our arms, and had a traditional dinner in the desert. Other excursions included a trip to Hatta Dam, a water reservoir in the middle of a beautiful mountain range, and a visit to the beach. With the same sense of awe I had viewing Dubai from 124 floors in the air, I was in awe of the natural beauty of the country.

Two highlights of the trip were our excursions to Abu Dhabi and Global Village. Global Village is a real-life Epcot, where ninety different nations from all over the world have outdoor bazaars full of their goods, crafts, and trinkets. I visited the Pakistani display and truly felt like I was walking the streets of Lahore again while also buying Yemeni honey and shopping for lamps in Turkey. It was an amazing blend of cultures and coexistence. My classmates and I loved Global Village so much that we asked to go back a second time the night before we departed to buy more souvenirs to bring home. We even attended a live performance by Jay Sean.

Before this trip, the Arab world was entirely unknown to me beyond the Western media's skewed depictions of conflict and war in the region. Walking around Dubai, with all of its opulence on full display, was an interesting experience, to say the least, but there was also a balance of traditional culture, foods, and goods that I realized only after seeing it myself.

Botswana

It came as no surprise to anyone who knew me that, following graduation, I wanted to go abroad. I applied for both a Fulbright scholarship and to the Peace Corps. I made it to the semi-finalist round of a Fulbright scholarship to teach English in South Africa but ultimately did not receive a finalist spot. Although I was upset at the time, hoping to return to a country that was extremely formative in my college career, I found out while I was in the UAE for spring break that I was accepted by the Peace Corps. So, after graduation, in July 2019, I packed up my belongings in two suitcases and headed to Botswana for a service term of twenty-seven months.

Botswana is a middle-income, land-locked country bordered by South Africa, Namibia, Zimbabwe, and Zambia. I chose this program specifically because volunteers worked with communities across Botswana to achieve an HIV-free generation through working in schools, nongovernmental organizations, health clinics, and district offices. Having just graduated with a degree in global health and development, I was eager to get some hands-on experience doing just that.

Upon arriving, we stayed for a week in Gaborone, the capital city, to get basic training on language, the historical context of the country, and broad overviews of the programming. Every day around 10 A.M., we would take a break for tea, which is a custom across the country that I loved very much as it reminded me the house in Pakistan where I grew up and where everything revolved around cups of tea. I was assigned to work alongside the and guidance and counseling teacher to help implement strategies for life-skills education involving safe and healthy relationships, career coaching, and more. My community of Kalamare had not had a volunteer for six years or so and was eager to have me around to help facilitate community gatherings and convenings for the students.

However, all of this came to a standstill in March 2020 when COVID-19 hit. Botswana was one of the last nations in the world to have a positive case, and by the end of February 2020, we were doing lessons at school on how to stay healthy. However, there was a global evacuation of Peace Corps volunteers, and unfortunately, almost as quickly as I packed my bags to go to Botswana, I packed them to return home. At the time, a lot of us thought we would return to our service, so I said many "see you laters" rather than proper "goodbyes." I will never forget the kindness and community I was shown even though I did not fulfill my full service commitment.

Throughout the eight months I was in Botswana, I met some of the most amazing people, had some of the most incredible moments of my life, and was constantly surrounded by natural beauty. This experience challenged me in many ways but it also helped me understand what it meant to be a citizen of the world. In Setswana, there is a saying, "*motho ke motho ka batho*," which translates to, "I am because we are," and it captures succinctly how we are all interconnected as one. I will forever be a better version of myself because of the incredible people, experiences, and personal growth I experienced during my time in Botswana.

It is difficult to fully capture what my study abroad experiences mean to me and how they have transformed me into the person I am today; however, I will try to sum it up in a few sentences.

Studying abroad has not only made me more resilient and adaptable, it has made me significantly more compassionate. Having experienced total strangers open their homes, culture, and traditions to me all over the world is such a beautiful thing that I hope to reciprocate. Even when I couldn't fluently speak the language, I learned to communicate through food, laughter, smiles, and other universal human experiences. Studying abroad has not only made me a better, more empathetic traveler, it has made me a better, more empathetic human.

It was fascinating to me how I could be in South Africa but eat food at a restaurant that reminded me of home or experience a version of the concept of *ummah* in Botswana. My definitions of "home" and "family" have expanded as I now have homes and families in multiple places around the world. If asked, "Is there anything you would do differently if given the chance?," my response would simply be that I wish I had studied abroad sooner, more frequently, and for longer durations during my undergrad experience.

One of my misconceptions was that studying abroad was only for those who could financially afford it, but my university had plenty of options where financial aid could partially or fully cover the costs. Blogs and YouTube videos of people explaining their study abroad journeys were helpful, especially when I was choosing where to serve in the Peace Corps.

Each experience pushed me to be more understanding, adaptable, and resilient as a citizen of the world. I have referenced anecdotes of each of my study abroad opportunities in job interviews, including in my work as the chief of the office of digital strategy at the White House. Each time, I have found it shows a unique, dynamic set of experiences that translate across so many fields. A huge amount of credit goes to Mercer for enabling me to study abroad multiple times, with each experience offering something entirely new and profound. *Even if you feel scared or nervous to step out of your comfort zone, know there is so much beauty and comfort in exchange with people, cultures, and traditions that you cannot fully learn just through textbooks.* Studying abroad and traveling has led me "home" to more places than I could imagine, and I am eternally grateful for that.

CATALYZED CRITICAL CONSCIOUSNESS

12

"TO HELL WITH GOOD INTENTIONS": HOW ASKING HARD QUESTIONS LED TO A CHANGE OF MIND

Chase Williams

Political Science, Environmental Policy and Spanish minors
Class of 2013

"If you can't live longer, live deeper."
—Italian Proverb

> "I am here to suggest that you voluntarily renounce exercising the power that being an American gives you. I am here to entreat you to freely, consciously, and humbly give up the legal right you have to impose your benevolence on Mexico. I am here to challenge you to recognize your inability, your powerlessness, and your incapacity to do the 'good' that you intended to do."
>
> —Ivan Illich

"To hell with good intentions." This is the key message Ivan Illich, an Austrian Roman Catholic priest, theologian, philosopher, and social critic, delivered to American volunteers gathered at the annual Conference on InterAmerican Student Projects in Cuernavaca, Mexico, in April 1968. More than fifty years later, it is a message that often finds its way into the curriculum of those preparing for community service, service learning, and study abroad.

Likely, your trusted Mercer professors have already assigned this short and important reading to you. If not, I recommend you take ten minutes right now to read it. It's easy to find online.

I first encountered Illich's address in the days leading up to a 2012 service learning and study abroad experience in Cape Town, South Africa. Admittedly, it was something that I moved to read quickly alongside a jam-packed syllabus of other readings in the lead-up to the trip. I remember it gave me pause for a few moments. There was an uncertain inkling of what it might mean to arrive and provide service to a community I'd never met in a place I'd never been with an immensely complex past and present. However, everything about the upcoming time abroad was already in motion. The flight tickets were purchased, the classes had begun, and the excitement was building. It was an important message, I thought, but perhaps it didn't necessarily apply to my upcoming experience. It felt easy enough to compartmentalize and move on.

We landed in South Africa a few days later. There were nearly a dozen Mercer students, including me, and two professors. For the majority of us, it was our first time in South Africa and our first time on the African continent. We now had two weeks together to advance our learning through two courses—one focused on the politics and developmental journey of South Africa, and the other on apartheid and postapartheid literature—and to complete a service project with a group of students at Hector Peterson Secondary School in Wallacedene, an informal housing settlement on the outskirts of Cape Town.

While the class and reading components of the trip were critical, the main feature was the service project. We were fortunate that the program had an established and trusted partnership with a small, local nonprofit organization working in Wallacedene that focused on providing extracurricular activities to schools in the area to build leadership skills and encourage stronger community bonds. Our service project paired with the drama club at Hector Peterson throughout our trip, with the ultimate goal of supporting and guiding the students in the club to perform a play for their community about their lived experiences in Wallacedene.

The Mercer group and the drama group came together tentatively at first. The majority of the drama students were in their early teenage years. With the nonprofit staff's direction, we spent our initial hours together in a big classroom at the school. These first moments were transformational for the Mercer group and me. We were welcomed into the community through the power of song. It's hard to say what shifted in the room at the outset, but from then on it was settled; we were connected. Each day, sharing in communal song would mark the beginning and end of our time together.

The relationships between the Mercer group and the drama group continued to deepen. One afternoon was particularly meaningful and concerning at the same time. Something called the "hot seat" was proposed by an older student serving as a guide to the drama group. It involved going around the room in a circle and sharing something very personal with everyone around you in service of forging deeper bonds. It was a powerful emotional space for the entire room. The concern came from some of the children sharing traumatic stories of sexual abuse and violence in a setting with limited psychosocial support. These were the bonds and experiences that the play was built upon.

As our time together in Cape Town drew to a close, we made it successfully to the day of the community performance, which was held at the school. Given the lived experiences in Wallacedene at the time, the drama group chose a performance centered on the themes of HIV and AIDS awareness, the dangers of sexual assault, and the power of education. It was well attended by community members around the school. When all was said and done, the students were proud of what they had created together and shared with their loved ones and neighbors. My honest assessment is that our

Mercer group was simply along for the ride at every step instead of leading the charge, as we may have thought.

It was incredibly difficult for me, at the end of the experience, to lose this brief but intense community that we had formed together, not just between the Mercer group and the drama group, but also within the Mercer group. We had swiftly bonded and almost just as quickly we were saying goodbye. In a collection of his short stories, David Eagleman reflects on this type of loss, writing, "A mood haunts actors on the drop of the final curtain: after months of working together, something greater than themselves has just died. After a store closes its doors on its final evening, or a congress wraps its final session, the participants amble away, feeling that they are part of something larger than themselves, something they intuit had a life even though they can't quite put a finger on it."

In the period after I returned home from Cape Town, I found myself on a path that was motivated by a desire to reverse that feeling of loss and to seek out a new community in service of others. I was heading into my senior year and needed to have a firm plan in hand. I was inspired to make an ill-fated attempt to apply for a Fulbright scholarship in South Africa, which led to a fortunate series of events that brought me to northern Thailand immediately after graduation, where I spent a year teaching English for a small, local nonprofit organization. As these things can sometimes go, my time in Thailand then brought me to Colombia to work with yet another small, local nonprofit organization supporting rural communities through ecotourism. The good intentions continued and were fueled by an eagerness to be out in the world after spending my whole life in the state of Georgia.

It was here that I started channeling my interest in the field of international development. My understanding then was that this was a career that valued a graduate degree as an important accolade. With that in mind, I optimized for speed, high brand recognition, and interesting location by completing a master of science in international development from the London School of Economics. While there I became fascinated by the nexus between international development and humanitarian response, especially related to climate-driven disasters amid the climate crisis.

One of the biggest lightbulb moments for me throughout that journey, which built on the experience in South Africa, was that local communities and local nonprofit organizations are best positioned to solve their communities' challenges. With this in mind, following graduation I accepted a role in Washington, DC, at GlobalGiving, a trusted nonprofit dedicated to accelerating community-led change around the world. It has now been nearly seven and a half years since I joined GlobalGiving. In my time at the organization, I have helped to create a disaster response team and now manage more than $50 million in flexible grant-making funds for local organizations on the front lines of crisis and disaster response in more than 170 countries. Our mantra is that local communities closest to the problems are also closest to the solutions. We simply need to properly resource local community organizations around the world.

All of this flowed from those meaningful feelings of connection that were driven by the understanding and trust of that local nonprofit partner when my Mercer group first arrived in South Africa.

With more than a decade of distance since that time in South Africa, I can say that Ivan Illich's words feel heavier and aren't as easily dismissed. There are a lot of hard questions to answer about my experience there. Some of them can be shocking and can feel crude—isn't it true that the drama group may have been better served if we had donated directly to the school the value of twelve Mercer students' worth of airfare from the US? Should we have asked the drama group students to share vulnerable and traumatic stories? What "damage" might have occurred without any psychosocial specialists on hand? Is the service learning a success because I went through my transformations? Did these transformations come at the expense of using the drama group students as tools? These are not easy questions. What Illich describes in his address is the immense risk that can manifest within a global system that is deeply inequitable and unjust, rendering communities around the world as either helpers or those in need of help (or not even worthy of being helped).

As you consider your study abroad experience, *I encourage you to listen to the local community members around you. Do not hold onto your initial expectations or judgments tightly. Be ready and willing to change your mind. Have a bias to listening instead of a bias to telling.* My time in South Africa taught me so much and directly shaped who I am today. More than anything else, I have taken away the fact that I do not know nearly as much as I think I do, and the only way I can make meaningful change in this world is by working collaboratively with those in the local communities that have lived experience.

The world's challenges are immense. The solutions to these challenges demand connection and solidarity. How we go about making those connections and expressing that solidarity truly matters. As you consider your plans to experience the world around you and to contribute to solutions, I encourage you to reflect deeply on Illich's cautionary message and urgent plea. In all that we do, let's interrogate our good intentions.

13

A LIFELONG LEARNER

Laurel McCormack

Major: International Affairs
Minor: Photography
Class of 2012

"People get to know one another when traveling."
—Bantu Proverb

I felt carsick and utterly entranced as the bus wound its way through and down the mountains of Parque Nacional el Tepozteco, from Ciudad de México (CDMX) into Cuernavaca. Two national parks and a standing guard of volcanic mountains separate Cuernavaca from CDMX. Once I had the chance to explore the city from all angles, I realized that the mountains climb in every direction with the city nestled in the middle, giving me a feeling both of expansiveness and protection.

I made this trip from CDMX to Cuernavaca for the second time in as many years. I was returning to stay with a host family and take Spanish language classes on social and environmental justice issues affecting low-income, Indigenous, and LGBTQ+ people in Mexico. As our bus descended into the city, I remembered another bus ride, twelve years earlier, on my way to study at Hong Kong Baptist University (HKBU) as an undergraduate student. I had not known when I arrived at the airport that only a fourth of the land in Hong Kong, a special administrative region of China, is developed. As we passed fishing villages and green hills on our way to the city center, I gaped with wonder.

In the coming months, newly made friends would beckon me to explore the islands, ridges, and coasts that make up the country of Mexico. I've come to realize that studying in another country means being open to learning about the land itself as well as from friends and teachers. In those places and with those people, far from home, I have learned an eclectic but critical set of lessons about accepting generosity and being generous, about understanding United States cultural values and hegemony through other lenses, and about being a lifelong student. These lessons are better shared as vignettes, moving between my experiences in Hong Kong and Cuernavaca to etch the impact they have had on my character and my path over the past twelve years since graduating from Mercer University.

Generosity

Growing up, I was the oldest child of parents who strove to push our family from the working class to the middle class by the time I left for college. While I always had what I needed, I was often stressed while studying at Mercer about covering my costs. I felt pinched for time, too. Between classes, campus odd jobs, and student groups, I stretched myself thin. In Hong Kong, however, the group of friends I made showed me how to share resources and time in a way that has continued to shape how I connect with others.

By the time I arrived in Hong Kong, I had decided two things: first, I would stick close to a friend who was the only other Mercer student at HKBU that semester, and second, I would try to meet students from places I knew little about, rather than stay comfortable in the group of American exchange students. During the first week, my Mercer friend and I met two journalism students from Singapore and immediately hit it off. We began to hang out regularly and to invite new friends to join us on our adventures. Before long, our friend group grew to include South Korean, Malaysian-

Australian, Hong Kongese, and mainland Chinese folks. We shared zany senses of humor and a love for scouting out good food, but we were otherwise very different people who came together hoping for connection and companionship in a new place. These friends taught me to order shared family-style meals when we ate out and argued over who would buy our desserts on late-night adventures. More importantly, they would drop everything to spend time together, even when classwork piled up. They were masters of deeply listening to one another and of sharing, in return, about themselves, their countries, and their hopes for the future.

One weekend, we set out as a group for Tap Mun, a fishing village on an island off the northeast coast of Hong Kong. We spent that day walking along the shoreline and chatting with the town elders over lunch at a small seafood restaurant. The elders told us about how their town's young people were being forced to move to the city center to find work and how the community was struggling to maintain its local traditions and economy without its youth. Day tourists like us brought some cash into the village but did little to restore what had been lost in Hong Kong's move towards urban development, which came at the expense of smaller towns that valued more traditional ways of community living. We traded stories with the elders and then went on our way, only leaving for Hong Kong by ferry when night began to fall.

When we got back, a friend realized with dismay that she had left her wallet on the dock at Tap Mun and would have to return to search for it. Another friend decided without a second thought that he would take the last ferry back to the island with her. I huffily decided to accompany them, though with immense concern about whether we would get back to Hong Kong in an affordable way after the public ferries stopped running. As we navigated back to Tap Mun, my friend hung her head on the deck banister, feeling awful for diverting our evening plans. I realized my preoccupation with not having enough time or money was keeping me from responding kindly to my friend in a time of need.

We began to joke with our friend to lighten her spirits, and when we got back to the Tap Mun pier, we spotted her wallet immediately. We found a jet taxi willing to take us back to Hong Kong, and wouldn't let our friend open her wallet to help us pay. The three of us huddled together as we sped back over the water, staring up at a star-studded sky that had been obscured from us since our arrival in the light-polluted city center. I have often thought of that night as the turning point when I realized that counting pennies and minutes spent with friends only made me more isolated and anxious. Following my friends' examples of generously sharing time, care, and resources led me to feel more connected and uninhibited.

I have tried in the eleven years since that semester to share what I have as generously as possible, including in my work with refugee and immigrant families and youth. I helped create and run programs that connect newcomers and longstanding community members to fuel mutual cultural exchange and open pathways to accessing needed resources and decision-making power. Larger possibilities—of friendship, community-building, and even systems change—seem to present themselves when we share time and resources across cultural differences.

The United States through Other Lenses

Spending time in Hong Kong and Cuernavaca—places with values different from those of the US— I witnessed firsthand the impact of US policies, which has reshaped my view of my own country and inherited culture. I have tried to paint a small portrait of the mutual care and resource-sharing that characterized my HKBU friend group. At Cuernavaca, where I was studying Spanish for the second time, I once again found myself surrounded by folks who were especially community-minded. I studied at a language school called Centro Internacional de Lenguas, Arte, y Cultura- Paulo Freire

(CILAC), which has been tied for decades to social justice movements in Mexico and Central America and was hosted by Ángeles and Fernando, an older couple with an incredible history of supporting grassroots change at local, national, and transnational levels.

My friends from HKBU and my hosts in Cuernavaca were, arguably, from cultures that broadly share an emphasis on the collective good over individual achievement. As an American, I struggle with cultural expectations that I should be independent and self-sufficient. I "should" work to provide for myself and become successful (i.e., to have a "good job" that pays well, to own my own house, and so on), and I largely expect everyone else to do likewise. My friends in Hong Kong and Cuernavaca, however, have modeled what it looks like to live less for individual gain and more with an eye toward familial duty, group cohesion, and community responsibility. Spending time in such "collectivist" groups jolts me into reexamining the cultural norms I have been socialized into in the US. Are we better off striving alone when economic, racial, social, and political systems are unfairly stacked, making it unlikely that most people will ever reach the standard American ideal of "success"?

My friends in Cuernavaca engage in activism out of a vision for the collective good in ways that drive home a critique of US systems, demonstrating that other ways of being together are possible. Solidarity with Indigenous pueblos binds together my CILAC teachers and host family. They have shared their experiences of becoming disenchanted with many political and social movements, only to find renewed hope in Indigenous movements such as the Ejército Zapatista de Liberación Nacional (EZLN).

The EZLN was formed in the 1980s by Indigenous peoples who rose up in the southern Mexican state of Chiapas to reclaim their right to belong to the land and to live autonomously from violent state and multinational corporate actors. Their Rebel Zapatista Autonomous Municipalities are collectively held, with all members participating in decision-making and the operation of their schools, health centers, farms, and businesses.

My hosts and teachers have each spent extensive time with Zapatista communities, beginning in the early 1990s after the EZLN declared autonomy on the eve of the enactment of the North American Free Trade Agreement (NAFTA). The Zapatistas rightly predicted that NAFTA would devastate the ability of rural Mexican communities to earn a fair wage from the corn, beans, and other produce they grew as they were forced to compete with US-subsidized products. This devastation is evident even to foreigners like me.

I spend the weekends riding buses to smaller pueblos outside of Cuernavaca, much like I did in Hong Kong. As we wind through the gorgeous mountains down into the fertile valleys of central Mexico, I see huge swaths of green fields with signs saying "*Se vende este terreno*"—this land is for sale. My teachers tell me that many rural Mexicans are buckling under decades of unfair trade with the US, forced to sell their best produce at a fraction of the fair price to US markets and are left with produce they cannot sell in a Mexican market flooded with cheap American produce. Many rural folks from this part of Mexico are forced to choose between staying and risking losing all they've built or migrating to a city in hopes of finding work (reminiscent of the youth from Tap Mun who were forced to leave their ancestral village to work in the city center). Some who leave take their chances at the Mexican-US border, where they face increasingly deadly conditions as US political parties compete to show who is "toughest on immigration."

Indigenous and rural collective responses to death-dealing Mexican and US policies are born under such high-pressure conditions. In a pueblo just south of Cuernavaca called Cuentepec, for example, the largely Indigenous Nahuatl-speaking community has spent years fighting the incursion of North American mining companies who want to drill for gold and silver in the mountains where the ancestors of Cuentepec families have lived for many centuries. My teachers explained that the mining practices these companies use in Mexico are banned in the US and Canada, in which incredibly hot water is used to separate dirt from possible gold particles, and then pumped back into waterways. The added chemicals and heat of the water kill plant and aquatic life and then begin to affect the land. People's health is affected as the water quality plummets. To address this, the people of Cuentepec have organized themselves. Adults in the pueblo run programs to teach their youth how to resist the mines through art, pride in their Nahuatl language and traditions, and care for the earth. The community also reaches out to surrounding pueblos to ask for help confronting the corporations.

My CILAC teachers and hosts have joined Cuentepec protests and community efforts, inspired by their cause to call for limits to the exploitation of the region's resources and people. While rural and Indigenous Mexican communities in Chiapas and Cuentepec continue to face daunting challenges, their creativity in organizing and working collectively to push back against individualistic advancement at all costs has contributed to my paradigm shift in values. My friends in Cuernavaca, in turn, teach me ways to be in solidarity with those we are connected to, even across national borders.

Life-long Learning Abroad

My time studying in Hong Kong and Cuernavaca, twelve years apart, has convinced me of the lasting value of leaving the country to learn from those who live and understand the world differently than I do. I remember realizing while in Hong Kong that my friends, who each lived half the world away from the US, knew far more about my country than I did about any of theirs. My time in Cuernavaca reinforced the fact that much of the world is forced to pay attention to what the US does as we seek an ever-widening expansion of our military, political, economic, and cultural power. Being an American citizen requires me to confront the uncomfortable truth that I often have immense privilege even when studying abroad in places where I may not know the language or culture.

A photography class assignment during my semester at HKBU provided a powerful example of this lesson. We were tasked with making short documentary-style videos in Kwun Tong, one of the last remaining traditional neighborhoods in the area, which was about to be torn down and reconstructed as the zone quickly gentrified. I was the only white student and one of two foreign students in a class otherwise made up of students from Hong Kong.

We set out that morning and split up once we reached the crowded marketplace, each person finding a spot to record. I snooped deep into an alley of small shops and stopped at the entryway of a locksmith shop, where an elderly, kind-faced man was busy cutting key copies. I pointed to my camera, and when he didn't say anything in reply, began to film, smiling a few minutes later when he stopped working long enough to say a couple of sentences I could not understand. I filmed a little longer, thanked him using one of the only Cantonese phrases I had learned, and headed back to meet my class. I congratulated myself on getting such a good shot, not having seen any other group members in that part of the market.

Later in class, we took turns showing our videos and giving critiques. I proudly hit play on my video, then felt my heart stop as the class burst out laughing when the locksmith spoke to me in Cantonese. My professor turned to me, smiling gently, and told me, "This gentleman said he wanted you to leave but didn't know how to tell you in English." I was mortified. My classmates shared that they had tried filming in that part of the market only to be shooed away. It dawned on me that my whiteness and foreigner/non-Cantonese-speaking status had likely given me access to a place I should not have been, where even my Hong Kong-born peers were outsiders. When I travel as an American citizen, as a white person, or as a college-educated person, I am likely granted a certain set of privileges in many parts of the world because of the very systems of American hegemony discussed above.

I have tried to be aware while studying in Cuernavaca of the differences in identity and power held between me and my hosts. I came to an adult language school hoping to be a learner among people who not only consented to, but were eager for, cultural exchange, and who would be compensated fairly for teaching and hosting me. As Ángeles told me when I chose to return to study at CILAC, "I don't host students as a business. I love the way we discuss politics, religion, everything. Students become family. But still, it helps us to be paid by the school when students come." One might think that the differences in nationality, class, and background between me and my hosts would make meaningful friendships difficult, but I have found that folks in explicitly cross-cultural spaces are often glad to talk openly about differences in our identities and the societies that formed us. From there, friendships seem to grow more honestly and richly, with room for discovering what binds us together. I hope to continue being a student of our human differences and similarities, in places far from home, for the rest of my life.

Leaning into these differences and similarities has transformed me in lasting ways. My friends in Hong Kong and Cuernavaca taught me to be a more generous person. I learned with them to give my time, care, knowledge, and resources with a trust that living and sharing in a community will make one far richer than worriedly hoarding in isolation. My friends and hosts also imbued in me a critical consciousness to notice and question the American cultural norms I had previously accepted without question. I have become a more reflective person, able to trace both my privileges and responsibilities as an American in a world scarred by the impact of US neo-imperialism. One of those privileges, for example, was living most of my life as a monolingual English speaker. When I committed to (finally) learning a second language as an adult, my humility and curiosity grew as I stumbled to express myself in others' terms. Yet I also realized with gratification that I could better understand my friends' own worldviews and cultural backgrounds when we conversed in their first language.

There are many ways to expand on our learning after returning home. We can continue or even begin foreign language study, motivated by a new appreciation for its utility and beauty. We can seek to support justice movements for people and for the land, even across borders, by joining solidarity organizations and volunteering our time to raise awareness about critical issues in the country where we studied. We can even start as simply as buying fair trade goods from that country instead of from big box stores. Perhaps most importantly, we can maintain the connections to friends and hosts made while studying abroad, and even deepen them over time. The perspective gained from years of sustained connection to another country sharpens our self-introspection and cross-cultural communication skills, which are critical in any workplace or community in our increasingly interconnected world.

Tips and Strategies

- Open yourself to forming friendships with people who may seem very different from you, and not just with those you can immediately relate to.
- Offer your time, care, and resources just as generously in return.
- Get to know the history of the land on which you will walk, and of the people who have long defended it, especially if that land has been colonized or exploited by far-away states and corporations.
- Take notice of different cultural values in your friends and hosts, and use the opportunity to reflect on the values you have been taught in your home culture.
- Take note of your home country's systems—the military, economic, political, and social policies and practices used—and what role they have had in shaping the world, for better or worse.
- Discover any collective activism or mutual aid happening in your host school or community, and find out what kinds of changes are

being achieved through such efforts. You never know what tips for living differently alongside others you might pick up and bring back to incorporate into your life at home!

- Bravely acknowledge differences in identity between you and your hosts, including the privileges and disadvantages that you each face in cross-cultural encounters.
- Come home eager to find ways to stay in touch with and nurture the connections you made with your host community.
- Be a forever student of ways we can better connect across differences to alter systems and allocate resources for the benefit of the collective good, as defined by your chosen communities, both near and far.

14

FROM "INTENDING TO HELP" TO REALIZING WORTH AND CURATING SUSTAINABLE IMPACT

Amirah Houry

Political Science (Georgia State University)
Class of 2015

"The world is the traveler's inn."
—Afghan Proverb

On May 22, 2010, I joined a group of sixteen Mercer students and faculty for a month-long Mercer on Mission trip to Cape Town, South Africa (MOMSA). In partnership with EMEP (Extra Mural Education Project), a Ministry of Education-funded NGO, we worked with twenty-three tenth- and eleventh-grade students in the Wallacedene township to write and perform a play that reflects the experiences of the current generation of young people of South Africa. The play, "The Hot Seat: Untold Stories of a South African Township," dealt with issues like hunger, parental abandonment, domestic abuse, poverty, AIDS, rape, and gangs. The project involved reading South African-authored plays with the township "learners," helping them conceive of their subjects for monologues, write and revise the monologues, and block and perform the play before an audience of parents, teachers, and community members.

Fortunate enough to have my father co-leading the trip, I saw it as a brilliant opportunity to step out of my comfort zone and gain some "real world" experience before I entered my senior year of high school. The experience was truly transformative, exposing me to issues, conditions, and relations that profoundly affected my academic and career choices. I participated with the intent of "helping" the people of the township. *Implied was the sense that because I am educated and live in a relatively more affluent society, I had an informed sense of what the people of South Africa needed. That was patently false.* I, like many of my peers, had quite naively believed poverty to be the result of poorly managed financial systems or the lack of a robust jobs market. The reality is that the causes of poverty are multidimensional and so solutions must be led by the communities who understand these unique contexts and conditions.

As part of the MOMSA program, I was assigned to read *Kafka's Curse*, which provides a unique perspective on the psychological effects of apartheid on the nonwhite population through the lens of two Coloured Muslims living in a township in postapartheid South Africa. The main implication of the book by Achmat Dongor is that modern-day South Africa's systematic discrimination against those born in poverty has created a mental condition among the marginalized populace that undermines their self-worth and individualism. This conclusion lies in direct contrast to the anti-apartheid youth movement fueled by pride in heritage and hopefulness for a better future regardless of race.

The students I worked with in Cape Town showed me that they understood what was happening, and why it was happening, and were aware of some of the potential solutions to address the complex root causes of poverty that plagued black and brown communities across the country. They did not, however, have the resources and the means with which to exercise these ideas in the service of their communities. Over and over, they kept reassuring us that everything would be fine and that conditions were bound to improve. Just as young people were at the forefront of the apartheid liberation movement of the 1960s and 1970s, they were perceived as the future of a "better" South Africa.

My experiences in South Africa have been instrumental in shaping my career. Upon completing my undergraduate degree in international affairs, I joined Peace Corps Moldova, working in educational development in a small village for nearly three years. In Moldova, I witnessed a unique but similar reality to what I experienced in South Africa—young people living in poverty, their futures dictated by Moldova's inability to rein in corruption. My experience in South Africa and Moldova has allowed me to recognize that aid, as a charity, is unsustainable due to the scale and complexities of the conditions that perpetuate corruption, poverty, and inequality. Currently, I lead the European Individual Philanthropy Program at BRAC, a Southern-led NGO that provides women living in extreme poverty and climate-vulnerable conditions with the tools to help them raise themselves out of poverty. The fight against poverty must be done through the enabling and empowering of the local people so they can cultivate local solutions to a lingering problem—the notion of rich and poor is material at its core, but it is only one dimension of the concept of poverty.

Even though I have traveled around the world from a very young age, these educational experiences were genuinely transformative in every sense of the world. Going abroad on my own has taught me a great deal about myself, opened my eyes to the complexities of local, national, and international affairs, and has given me profound insight into understanding delicate issues such as identity, capacity, and impact. I want to urge, in the strongest possible terms, that every undergraduate student take advantage of studying abroad. The impact is both tangible and intangible, but also enduring. *Personally, I never felt the same after returning from Cape Town, and I am certain that both my personal life and academic career would have taken a very different course had it not been for this incredible journey.*

Talk to your academic advisor about the value of studying or interning abroad, make an appointment to consult with study abroad advisors, and familiarize yourself with all the financial support available to American students wishing to travel and experience the world firsthand. If the resolve is there to pursue study abroad, no obstacle is too large to overcome. *Just do it!*

PURPOSE AND CALLING

15

FROM SOUTH AFRICA TO SELF-DISCOVERY: HOW MY STUDY ABROAD EXPERIENCE DEFINED MY PURPOSE

Macire Aribot

International Affairs and Global Development Studies
Class of 2019

"We are all visitors to this time, this place we are just passing through. Our purpose here is to observe, to learn, to grow, to love, and then we return home."
—Australian Aboriginal Proverb

"I am the daughter of Africa, and I say to you, fellow Africans, let us claim our right to dignity."
—Siolise

As a junior studying international affairs and global development studies at Mercer University, I had the opportunity to study abroad through the Mercer on Mission program to Cape Town, South Africa. The trip to South Africa was a unique experience for me as a Black girl who grew up in the US South with immigrant parents from Conakry, Guinea. Although I had traveled to West Africa previously, this would be a chance for me to gain greater exposure to the diverse cultures across the continent and pique my interest in solving African development challenges. It was the first time I would visit a country so similar to the United States in terms of its history of apartheid and deep racial divides, yet so different culturally and geographically. My positionality served as the basis for how I would navigate the journey and how I would remember it. It was in South Africa that I discovered my passion for social justice and the liberation of African and indigenous peoples.

Mercer on Mission's international service learning experience allowed me to travel across the world to learn about the history of settler colonialism, the challenges of apartheid, and the long journey toward freedom for South Africans who had experienced these events firsthand. The experience was unlike anything I had ever imagined, challenging me to broaden my horizons, helping me to understand my purpose in life, and setting me on a path to achieve new heights throughout my career.

When we landed in Cape Town on May 8, 2018, I immediately noticed the stark inequalities throughout the city. In a country barely thirty years freed from apartheid, the legacies of racial discrimination, displacement, and exploitation could be seen as we drove past townships and into the downtown area, with its million-dollar homes and thriving businesses. There were sixteen of us on the trip, including my professors, Dr. Houry, Dr. Morgan, and Dr. Nelson. We came from different backgrounds, representing the United States, India, Pakistan, Germany, Guinea, and more. For the next three weeks, I worked alongside my classmates in the local townships of Khayelitsha and Wallacedene at Hector Peterson Secondary School, Luhlaza Secondary School, and Pelican Park Primary School. At the primary school, we worked with teachers to help tutor students, and at the secondary schools, we worked with their debate teams to teach them about the United Nations and host a Model UN conference. As part of our learning experience, we took two courses: Post-Apartheid Transitions in South Africa and Understanding Race, Gender, and Ethnicity in South Africa. We also engaged with the local community through historical site visits, interactive presentations, and group discussions with local teachers and University of Cape Town students. Each day brought new challenges and opportunities for us to learn and grow. We delved deeper into the environment around us, studying its history and learning from community members striving to create a better place for all South Africans.

Throughout my time there, I learned about the root causes behind current issues of economic inequality, poor access to education and healthcare, land redistribution, unemployment, and poverty. Systemic racism is a significant factor exacerbating such challenges for Black and Coloured (mixed-race) populations living in South Africa. Since the early colonial settlements of Europeans dating back to the seventeenth century, British and Dutch colonialists imposed racially discriminatory laws that segregated and oppressed indigenous African (Bantu and Khoisan) and Asian populations. For example, in 1913, the British colonial power established the Natives Land Act of 1913, forcibly removing native Africans from land they had owned or worked for generations. They allocated only 7.5 percent of the land to natives and the rest to white European settlers. In 1948, the white-majority South African government implemented the system of apartheid, a highly institutionalized form of racial segregation and white supremacy.* This led to legislation that reinforced longstanding systems of oppression, such as limiting Black South Africans to education in domestic work, categorizing rights and privileges based on race (white, Coloured, Indian, or Black), and restricting movement and residence of nonwhite groups to townships.

The apartheid system continued for more than forty-five years. It ended with the leadership of freedom fighters such as Winnie and Nelson Mandela, Steve Biko, Solomon Mahlangu, and many others. I recognized these parallels with the Black experience in the United States. In the nineteenth and twentieth centuries, legislation

* "Land, Labour and Apartheid," South African History Online: www.sahistory.org.za/article/land-labour-and-apartheid. Accessed October 22, 2023.

such as the Jim Crow laws institutionalized anti-Black racism and segregation. As a result, Black communities were excluded from equal education, employment, and voting rights and subjected to violence from white people and white supremacist groups. With the leadership of civil and human rights activists such as W. E. B. Dubois, Martin L. King, Malcolm X, Fannie Lou Hamer, and many others, Americans saw the end of explicitly racist policies. However, just as with apartheid, the legacies of segregation and white supremacy still exist and hinder progress toward social and economic equity for all races.

Ultimately, we learned from our experiences tutoring students and listening to teachers' experiences that the impact of apartheid and postapartheid policies continues to negatively affect the development of Black and Coloured communities. Young students bear the brunt of these challenges due to poor education reforms and severely under-resourced schools. While tutoring at the primary and secondary schools, we saw directly how South Africa's history affected the students we worked with and how these negative effects would carry on postgraduation. For instance, during our first week, my classmate and I went into a mathematics classroom at Hector Peterson to observe and help the teacher as needed. To my surprise, we ended up teaching the entire class that period. The classroom was crowded with forty to fifty students, and due to the lack of desks or chairs, several students had to stand at the back. I remember being shocked that the teacher would so readily hand over her class to us, as I was initially uncomfortable because we were not math teachers. I quickly recognized that because we were "Americans," there was an expectation that we were more qualified than we were. This experience shed light on the prevailing notion of Western superiority, where Americans frequently assume a position of knowledge and authority, reinforcing subconscious beliefs in Western supremacy. However, the teacher, grateful for our help, moved to the back of the class and watched us as we spontaneously taught a lesson on "like terms" and "unlike terms." Despite successfully explaining the concepts, I thought to myself how unsustainable this was and how it illustrated the greater systemic challenges that manifested into overfilled classrooms where teachers are overwhelmed and students cannot learn in a healthy environment. In the long term, these barriers would create mounting difficulties for students and affect their ability to achieve postgraduation.

I also remember speaking to a nineteen-year-old student, Wonga, who recently graduated from Hector Peterson Secondary School. Wonga dreamed of attending the University of Cape Town and becoming a teacher. He had not been accepted yet due to issues with his application, but he spent time there as an intern to help younger students. Throughout our conversation, he shared with me that many students couldn't read and write and that using a computer was completely foreign to them. He also feared that many would never be able to leave the townships because of the failed school system and the lack of support at home. This showed how the same system that failed the previous generation would continue a cycle detrimental to future generations.

Despite South Africans' difficulties, there was a strong and deep sense of strength and determination to succeed, a sentiment that all Africans on the continent and across the diaspora understood. While working with the debate teams for the Model UN conference, I was inspired by their ambition, intelligence, and leadership. They were fast learners and naturally took on the role of diplomacy, debating important global issues they felt passionate about. The conference we organized was a success and left students proud of themselves and their accomplishments. It was the highlight of my experience because not only did I play a part in teaching them something new, but they also played a significant part in helping me find my voice and discover my leadership skills. I was intentional about every interaction because I saw myself in them and understood what it was like to be in their shoes. I focused on giving them the attention and encouragement I needed at their age.

Outside the lessons, we shared stories about our lives and taught each other childhood games and songs. They showed me how to *gwara gwara*, a popular South African dance at the time. We also shared poems, and after listening to a poem written by Siolise, a debate student, I realized that the students' and my fates were linked.

She recited, "Dignity to everyone who lives in Africa. Dignity to everyone who loves Africa. Hear my cry; let us love and respect each other; let us communicate and make good decisions. I have passion for my people, passion for my continent, passion for my culture. I am the daughter of Africa, and I say to you, fellow Africans, let us claim our right to dignity."

At that moment, I knew that after leaving South Africa and returning to my home in the United States I would have to do my part in addressing the persistent inequalities facing African and African descent communities. I made it my mission that students like Siolise, Wonga, and myself could achieve the dreams we envisioned for ourselves and our communities.

After returning to Mercer, my study abroad experience in South Africa became a guiding force. The lens through which I viewed the world had shifted, giving me a deeper sense of purpose and commitment to understanding global inequalities. I took courses on poverty alleviation models, global health, economics, and cultural anthropology. By the following summer, I participated in the Public Policy and International Affairs Junior Summer Institute (PPIA) at Carnegie Mellon University. I immersed myself in graduate-level international and domestic policy and economics courses there. These experiences refined my skills in policy analysis and deepened my understanding of social policies aimed at reducing poverty in the United States and abroad.

Following my early graduation, I ventured into the heart of policymaking, interning on Capitol Hill with the Congressional Black

Caucus Foundation. I later worked at the National Democratic Institute, focusing on Central and West Africa and Southern and East Africa to expand my knowledge of the challenges faced across African regions. In the wake of the 2020 global Black Lives Matter movement, I cofounded NoirUnited International, a global development and humanitarian organization focused on addressing emerging challenges facing African and African descent communities. What I learned through these endeavors was the magnitude of the work I had set out to do, and I quickly realized that further education would be essential. Encouraged by the professors who led my trip to South Africa, in 2021 I began my master of international affairs program at Columbia University's School of International and Public Affairs, where I concentrated on economic and political development, specializing in the African region. Here, I sharpened my understanding of development and honed my leadership skills. I got the opportunity to travel abroad to Kenya for my final capstone project to consult for the United Nations International Children's Emergency Fund (UNICEF) and work with government officials and civil society to support youth entrepreneurs. The experience I gained from my graduate program allowed me to fully dedicate myself to NoirUnited's Mission. It also led me to embark on a mission to the borders of Ukraine to advocate for and provide humanitarian assistance to more than a thousand African students who faced racial discrimination while fleeing the war.

Looking back, I see how my study abroad experience propelled me into a life of purpose and action. The chapters of my life unfolded in unexpected and incredible ways after my study abroad experience. It enabled me to envision a future where equity transcends borders, where every student is protected against discrimination and has the tools to develop their community in their image. My journey—from South Africa's townships to the halls of Columbia University—illustrates the profound impact of international education. It equipped me with knowledge and the compassion, determination, and confidence to confront global challenges head-on.

I entered Mercer University as a young girl eager to challenge myself to overcome my fears and take advantage of every opportunity that came my way. If I could do my college experience again, I would study abroad sooner, more often, and for a longer period to fully immerse myself in the community and culture of a new environment. However, the reality is that there are financial barriers for low-income students that limit access to study abroad. As a Pell Grant recipient myself, this was a major concern for me and played a role in my decisions. I later learned that undergraduate students can receive full scholarships to travel abroad and study new topics, learn critical languages, intern with local organizations, or conduct research on important issues. These programs include the Gilman Scholarship Program and the Critical Language Scholarship (CLS) Program. I would have taken greater advantage of these options to gain access to more opportunities in international education. Studying abroad was one of the best decisions I made as a student, and I believe that everyone, if given the opportunity, should embrace the experience of understanding their own identity and positionality in the world while unlocking the immense potential within themselves.

My advice to students interested in studying abroad would be to consider the following:

- "Just Do It."
- Never be afraid to step outside your comfort zone and take risks, as you may uncover profound insights about yourself during your journey.
- When you decide to take that step, choose a location that interests you, fully embrace the experience, and be open to learning from diverse perspectives.
- Ask questions, build relationships with the people you meet, and find ways to make a sustained impact on the community. After

studying abroad, you will find that your experiences have prepared you for the career path you're looking to enter or the graduate program you're hoping to pursue.

- Recognize that leveraging your study abroad experience is not only about advancing in your career, but also about creating bridges between cultures and using what you've learned to make a positive impact on the communities that have poured into you along the way. By expanding your cultural awareness, adaptability in diverse environments, and communication skills, you will develop the tools necessary to thrive and take actionable steps toward a more just and equitable global society. The memories you make abroad are ones that you will carry with you for the rest of your life and will serve as a reminder of how far you've come on your journey.

16

A NEWFOUND PASSION: HOW MY TRIP ABROAD INSPIRED A CHANGE OF CAREER PLANS

Colleen Closson

International Affairs, Global Health Studies
Class of 2016

"A traveler to distant places should make no enemies."
—Nigerian Proverb

I always knew that I wanted to study abroad. I chose Mercer University in part because of the Mercer on Mission program and its wide range of semester abroad options. However, when it came to choosing where to go, I was at a loss. There were so many places to visit and so many paths to choose from. Fortunately, Dr. Eimad Houry, my advisor, helped me channel this indecisive energy into focus.

I am not sure what first interested me in South Africa. As a double major in international affairs and southern studies, the parallels between South Africa and the American South were undeniable. Legally, Jim Crow and apartheid were over, but their effects continued to linger, and I wanted to learn more. As a result, the summer after my sophomore year, I spent a month with Mercer on Mission, exploring the country with a group of people whom I normally would not have spent much time with. As so many of us know, Mercer can often feel a bit like high school, with cliques that make it difficult to bridge the gaps between us. That summer, the lens of my life widened, and it was sobering to get to know so many of my classmates in ways I hadn't before. In learning more about the lives of South Africans, I also learned about my classmates' lives and the reasons they chose to join the trip that summer.

During our summer, we stayed in a bed and breakfast, and almost every night we would gather in the living room to debrief from our day; there was a lot to unpack, with many different opinions in the room. One of the most valuable aspects of Mercer on Mission is that there were students from many different disciplines on the trip. As a result of the varied perspectives this provided, I never felt like there were right or wrong answers as we debated the history and effects of apartheid and how the South African government had handled its aftermath. I appreciated how the program forced us to think critically about what we had seen and experienced regarding racism, poverty, and inequality. I learned how to write meticulously, finding ways to fully express what I was seeing, thinking, and feeling during this time.

I would be lying if I said I remembered specific details of our projects during my time in South Africa. I do recall feeling that the work we had done during the trip paled in comparison to all we learned; some of the projects we completed left me feeling like our work was a modern-day extension of colonialism. Our trip to South Africa sparked my first realization of white privilege and white guilt. Although my understanding of these topics has radically changed since then, I began to understand my own life within the context of how international systems of power influence who gets to live affluently while others experience poverty.

Leaving South Africa that summer was sad, and I was overjoyed when, the following semester, Dr. Houry gave me the opportunity to return for a longer period. For close to three months, I would live independently in the heart of Cape Town. During the week, I would intern with a nongovernmental organization called Ikamva Labantu.

Ikamva provided health education to the townships surrounding Cape Town. Despite not being a global health major, I decided it was an opportunity to learn something new, to return to a city I adored, and to spend more time getting to know and understand a small slice of this country better.

Although a Mercer on Mission trip is a wonderful introduction to studying abroad, there is nothing quite like a full semester to cultivate a level of independence. In college, you are growing less dependent, but there is a safety net. I had to learn how to drive on a different side of the road, navigate around an unfamiliar city without GPS, and meet people in a country where I did not know the language. *I would never have guessed how instrumental this time would be, and it laid the framework for my life after college.*

Driving into the Khayelitsha township each day for the internship fully opened my eyes to the gap between wealth and utter, abject poverty. I lived in the heart of Cape Town, surrounded by beautiful restaurants, endless things to do and see, and gorgeous houses. During the commute, I would leave this area and then watch as the quality of life slowly diminished. Taking the highway exit into Khayelitsha felt like entering another world. People lived among ridged tin shacks, without modern amenities such as running water or HVAC systems. It often felt shameful to drive in, knowing that I would be leaving and returning to comparatively lavish settings.

If I had not worked at Ikamva Labantu that semester, I do not doubt that my professional career would look very different. I planned to go to law school after completing my undergraduate degree, knowing that my interests lie in public policy. I knew that I wanted to effect change in some way, but I did not know what that would look like. While at Ikamva, I worked with Monica, a community health worker. She was warm and hospitable and quickly gave me a Xhosa name (Monika!); she cared for me as if I were her child. I went with her to schools and centers for the elderly while she taught about healthy lifestyles and behaviors. Monica had no formal education, yet she was remarkably knowledgeable about the lifestyles within the township and how to communicate effectively with the people she taught. She introduced me to township residents (often by the Xhosa name she had chosen for me) and allowed me to provide education where I could. None of what I taught was groundbreaking information. I remember teaching the elderly how to prevent falls and ways to promote healthy eating and physical activity. The people around us were genuinely interested and seemed to absorb what we had to say.

One of the leaders at Ikamva was an older woman, and at first, based on her decorum and manner of moving through the world, I assumed she was a nun. However, she was a nurse. She was responsible for the education of the community health workers, who were, in turn, responsible for educating the people who lived in the townships on ways to promote their health and safety. When I learned that community health workers were largely responsible for improving the health indicators of South Africans in the townships post-apartheid, I was shocked. I remember thinking that education seemed like such a minor factor in making such a significant change. I realized that nurses were responsible for educating the community health workers, the vast majority of whom were like Monica and had no formal education.

Until then, I had thought that people who created vast, sweeping change were politicians or attorneys, people who sat in fancy offices and typed or debated and argued all day. When I realized that just a few nurses, with the power of education, had been responsible for improving the health and lifestyle of an entire country, I knew that my career trajectory had changed. I went home and sat down with Dr. Houry, attempting to find ways to blend my newfound passion for health, specifically health education, with my majors. My senior thesis compared the eugenics policies of South Africa and various Southern states, including Georgia, which allowed me to delve more deeply into health policies and their lasting effects. After graduation, I took night classes to obtain the science prerequisites needed for nursing school. Within a year, I began my studies at Emory University to become a registered nurse.

I continue to use the knowledge and skills I learned at Ikamva as I work as a bedside nurse at the Department of Veterans Affairs. A significant portion of my job involves educating people and motivating them to improve their health and change their lives. There are structural barriers to improving health, not to mention trauma and its far-reaching effects on the human body and psyche. But when I see a patient's eyes light up when I teach them something new about their diagnosis or a medication they take, I know that I have chosen the right career. I am proud to continue the legacy wrought by the nurses and community health workers in South Africa to make seemingly minute changes to people's lives while creating long-lasting change within the larger population.

17

A PEACE THAT TRANSCENDS BORDERS, CULTURES, AND LANGUAGES: EXAMINING THE RESETTLEMENT EXPERIENCE IN LISBON, PORTUGAL

McKenna Kaufman

International Affairs and Journalism
Class of 2023

"Your feet will bring you to where your heart is."
—Irish Proverb

The morning of our class's flight to Portugal, I regretted signing up for the trip.

Based on how anxious and overwhelmed I was, you would've thought I was being shipped off to Portugal, never to return. While the trip was only one week long, it was sandwiched between the last day of finals week and Mercer University's 2023 commencement ceremony. Amidst wrapping up my exams, moving out of my Macon apartment for the final time, and preparing to walk across the stage and accept my diploma, I had been frantically researching, applying, and interviewing for resettlement and migration advocacy jobs in my hometown of Nashville, Tennessee. After months of trying, graduation was a week away, and I still had no definitive post-graduation plans.

I was a nervous wreck.

"Why did I sign up for this?," I whined to my mom as I finished zipping up my suitcase in preparation to be driven to the airport. Going on an international trip while my life for the last four years was quickly approaching its conclusion felt daunting.

"You're going to be happy you went," she reassured me.

Our trip, while only a week long, would cover a lot of ground. Our class of thirteen had spent the spring semester studying migration patterns across the Middle East, North Africa, and Southern Europe in preparation for interacting with migrant populations firsthand during our week in Lisbon, Portugal. We discussed the different factors that push immigrants and forcibly displaced people to decide to pick up their lives and move to a foreign country. Dr. Obidoa highlighted the health complications immigrants and refugees encounter on their journeys, while Dr. Houry gave us the political context of significant mass migrations over the past several decades.

During my time as an international affairs and journalism student at Mercer, I became deeply interested in displacement and resettlement. The flexibility of my courses during my final two years at Mercer allowed me to write news stories highlighting the stories of immigrants, intern at a resettlement agency, and conduct long-term research about the public's perception of international migration. Dr. Obidoa and Dr. Houry had been meaningful mentors to me during each of these projects. The trip to Lisbon felt like the culmination of my undergraduate career.

I just wished I knew what to expect of my life after the trip was over.

Throughout our ten-hour flight to Lisbon my brain was working overtime analyzing each of my job applications and interviews before finally deciding to try to get some sleep. Still, panicked thoughts echoed through my mind as our flight made the final descent into Lisbon.

"It's normal to work a food service job after you graduate while you get on your feet," I told myself.

"It might be good for me to take a few months to regroup and figure out what I want my career to look like. Plenty of people end up working jobs that don't relate to their major. Plenty of people decide not to go to graduate school. I'll be fine."

My worried thoughts quickly slipped away as our class hit the ground running the moment we arrived in Lisbon. Located on the southeastern coast of Portugal, Lisbon offers beautiful views of the Atlantic Ocean paired with rows of tall, pastel-colored buildings adorned in the city's famous ceramic tiles. Historically, the city's coastal location made it a gateway for trade and migration, facilitating the arrival of immigrants and refugees from Africa, the Middle East, and Asia.

On our first day, we visited the Lisbon offices of the Jesuit Refugee Service (JRS), an international organization that provides social services like education, mental healthcare, and humanitarian aid to refugee populations. Our class was met by a stream of JRS staff members ranging from psychologists to public relations specialists to caseworkers, each playing a role in the intricate web of refugee resettlement. They welcomed us into their offices and gave us a tour of a housing facility for new arrivals before we sat down for a meal with some of the complex's residents. They generously served us lunch and talked to us about their experiences emigrating from countries such as Bangladesh, Venezuela, and Iraq.

At every stop on our trip through Lisbon, I was amazed by the hospitality shown to us by the new arrivals we interacted with. The group of refugee young adults we visited at a group home sent us back to our hotel with handfuls of lemons from the tree in their backyard. Members of a nonprofit group called the Lisbon Project, which focuses on providing new arrivals with a support system for fellow migrants in the city, were enthusiastic about including our class in shopping, preparing, and serving a meal for more than fifty people at their weekly community dinner. A former football player from Iraq named Mo took my classmates and me on a field trip to a Portuguese grocery store and guided us around the tight corners and narrow aisles with patience.

Despite the stories of hardship we heard daily from migrants of all backgrounds. The immigrants and refugees we encountered in Lisbon were eager to welcome us into their spaces and share parts of their lives with us. By the midpoint of the week, I was determined to focus my postgraduate career on improving the resettlement experience for new arrivals.

On our fourth night, I stood at the center of a crowded room, enveloped by the sound of an endless number of languages being spoken, food sizzling in the kitchen, and Arabic pop music trickling out of a speaker tucked in the corner of the room. I let the sights and sounds of the Lisbon Project wash over me as I became acutely aware of the exhaustion weighing on my shoulders and eyelids.

I felt my phone buzz in my back pocket as the day's emails and texts began to come through after hours without internet or cell service. I quickly glanced at the screen before my eyes landed on the subject line of one particular email.

Welcome to the team!

I felt my stomach drop and my heart start to race as I skimmed the first few lines of the message. It was from the resettlement agency I interned with the year prior.

"I wanted to let you know we have decided on the Employer Engagement Coordinator position—congratulations!," it read. "We hope you will accept—I am looking forward to working together and know you will make a great addition to our team!"

I didn't even finish the last sentence before I rushed over to my classmates and professors to share the news. After months of waiting and anticipating my next step after graduation, I felt the weight of social expectations and my increasingly intense jet lag lift off my chest.

"This trip has been so serendipitous," Dr. Obidoa said. "Everything came together for you to receive this news in this place." To celebrate, Dr. Houry took my classmates and me out for ice cream on our walk back to the hotel that night. My professors' mentorship is the highlight of my undergraduate career.

This trip to Lisbon was the culmination of my undergraduate career. And I was getting to celebrate this accomplishment with the people who were integral to making it a reality.

The remainder of the trip felt surreal and almost like a precursor to the next phase of my life. During the final three days of that life-changing week, we visited Portugal's High Commission for Migration, a local resettlement agency and the site of a memorial for victims of Portugal's colonial conquests. While anger bubbled up inside me as we listened to accounts of discrimination and inaccessible social services, I was ready to get to work.

I write this account of our transformative trip to Portugal after finishing another exhausting but rewarding week managing the employment program of one of Nashville's three local resettlement agencies. I have the privilege of assisting more than thirty of our community's newest members with finding jobs that promote their long-term career goals, offer them opportunities for upward mobility, and assist with making the transition to living in a new place easier. I get to make a new friend every day.

I love my job more than I could have ever anticipated, but that same anger I felt in Lisbon continues to simmer daily. I work within the confines of government-funded employment and cash assistance programming—meaning that the folks I work with are often given fewer than six months to achieve financial independence.

The average American may not understand how challenging that is, especially in a country where few workplaces provide support for new arrivals to thrive.

One major difference between the Portuguese resettlement program and its American counterpart is the how much less time US agencies have to provide new arrivals with social services. In Lisbon, the refugee service providers we spoke with were given an eighteen-month timeframe to help their clients achieve financial stability.

My team and I are lucky if we are given eight months to guide a newly arrived refugee through the job search while they also navigate a city with virtually no public transit and a brand-new language.

I am forced to work within a system that was not built for the people I come to work every day to help. I come home angry and with a sinking feeling in my stomach most days. But despite the long hours and the seemingly never-ending line of obstacles blocking my clients from achieving their goals in this country, there are still bright spots.

As in Lisbon, my clients are some of the most hospitable people I have ever met. Home visits have become one of the best parts of my day because once we get past discussions about budgeting, job applications, and health insurance, I can talk and laugh with people whom I might never have met otherwise.

I'll always remember sipping on Turkish coffee while my client from Syria showed me photos of the intricate hair-braiding services he offered during his time living in Jordan. I'll always remember organizing bus training for a family from Iran before their first day of work. I'll always remember my twenty-year-old client's eyes widening in shock as he found out I was twenty-two years old ("I thought you were a mom!," he exclaimed). And I'll always remember being introduced to my client from Congo's new kitten that he rescued from the sidewalk of his apartment complex. The kitten's name is Max. I'll never forget the solemn discussions that ended in laughter and the strangers who became an indispensable part of my new community.

Despite the frustrations and the uphill battles, I find solace in the connections I've begun to build and the small victories won along the way. My job isn't just about finding employment within the confines of a flawed system; it is about increasing access, fostering understanding, and creating a sense of belonging for our new neighbors. It is about creating spaces of peace and safety that transcend borders, cultures, and languages.

As I reflect on my trip to Lisbon and the past four months of working as the resettlement case worker I always wanted to be, I recognize that justice for immigrants and refugees is still yet to be realized in the United States and countries around the world.

I've heard countless stories from the individuals I work with recounting the hate they've encountered on their journey to resettlement as a migrant and an outsider in a new place. Many are shocked by how little opportunity the United States has to offer as they struggle to pay their mounting housing costs using a combination of food stamps, refugee cash assistance, and the meager wages their employer pays them.

The international community has not been built to respond to migration in a meaningful way; xenophobic attitudes, sparse social services, and the rush toward financial self-sufficiency make the road after resettlement long, exhausting, and discouraging. For these reasons, trips like our class trip to Lisbon are integral to changing this status quo. International travel challenges biases, destroys ignorance, and catalyzes advocacy.

How students apply their changed mindsets and newfound knowledge post-travel is a critical part of the transformation that study abroad fosters. The academic, professional, and personal momentum I carried with me in the months after our plane touched down at the Atlanta airport was infectious. Armed with a broader worldview and a greater sense of social responsibility, I graduated from Mercer University with a sense of urgency for the work I was preparing to do in refugee resettlement. *The biggest mistake students can make after their study abroad trip is losing this life-changing momentum. The fire lit under travelers can become the driving force behind crucial personal development.* The months following the conclusion of a study abroad trip are the perfect time to learn a new language, start a new internship or volunteer opportunity, begin a research project, organize a community engagement project, or take an intimidating course. *The familiarity with discomfort that students develop during study abroad is easily lost if not quickly channeled into a project or task that makes the world better.*

I would not be as prepared to succeed in my current role without the conversations I had with migrants and resettlement professionals in Portugal. I am more compassionate. More adaptable. More open-minded. A global education that encourages stepping outside your comfort zone to become a more empathetic community member is critical to building a young workforce and generation eager to effect change. I am so grateful to the mentors I've had as a young adult who have encouraged me to do just that. I'm grateful for our short-but-sweet week in May, which we spent wandering those pastel streets, watching history unfold before our eyes.

As usual, my mom was right. I'm happy I went on our trip to Lisbon.

My Tips and Strategies for Leveraging the Impact of Study Abroad

- Keep a travel journal. You will be surprised how quickly the little details of your trip escape your mind after you return. Take detailed notes and journal entries that recount the places you visited, what you discussed, your classmates' names, the names of the people you spoke with, and more! Take lots of photos to accompany your entries.
- Learn how to effectively communicate all you experienced, whether verbally, through writing, or art. Sharing your experience with your family, friends, peers and community or a larger audience makes the impact of your study abroad trip extend past just you and your class. As you apply for internships and jobs

postgraduation, the ability to coherently discuss your trip will be an asset for applications and interviews.

- Let the momentum of the trip carry you to greater things. Channel the excitement you feel into a larger project or cause. Get involved with a new internship,social justice movement, volunteer opportunity, club, course, research project, or language. Don't let this infectious momentum fall stagnant when you return to your daily routine.

18

HOW I FOUND MY CALLING: LIFE-SHAPING ENCOUNTERS IN THE MIDDLE EAST

David Stokes

International Affairs and Religion
Class of 2020

"He who returns from a journey is not the same as he who left."
—Chinese Proverb

When I first visited the campus of Mercer University for a college tour in 2015, I remember being amazed by the university's commitment to making study abroad a key component of its academic programs. It seemed that almost every presentation I attended made some mention of the numerous study abroad programs offered by the university, including faculty-led trips, semester-long student exchange programs with university partners abroad, internships, and Mercer on Mission programs. I chose to attend Mercer in no small part because of these opportunities, as I was eager to expand my engagement with the world. I began my studies at Mercer in 2016 intending to major in international affairs (with an emphasis on the Middle East and North Africa), but as a result of my participation in several different study abroad programs over the next four years, I eventually added a second major in religion and a minor in French.

I participated in six different study abroad programs during my four years of study at Mercer: the faculty-led Spring Break in Dubai in March 2018, the Mercer on Mission in Georgia in June and July 2018, the student exchange program with Al Akhawayn University in Morocco from August to December 2019, and a summer internship in South Africa from May to August 2019. The remaining two study abroad programs—Gateway KSA in Saudi Arabia in February and March 2018 and a summer semester at the American University in Beirut, Lebanon, from June to August 2018—were fulfilled independently of Mercer University, but it was my faculty advisor, Dr. Eimad Houry, who identified these programs for me and encouraged me to apply, and they contributed as much to my academic growth and undergraduate studies as the programs directly organized by Mercer.

As will be discussed below, each of the six different study abroad programs furnished me with new skills in cross-cultural communication and languages—Arabic and French— and expanded my academic interest from international affairs to also include narrative and identity formation, nationalism studies, and the Arab-Israeli conflict. They also provided practical experience living and working in a Middle Eastern and Islamic context, which has proven invaluable to my professional development as I currently live and work in Morocco as a youth development specialist with the US Peace Corps in partnership with the Moroccan Ministry of Youth, Culture, and Communication. I focus on youth development, sharing life skills, and the promotion of English-language education, and at the time of writing, I am almost halfway through my two years of service. I fervently believe that without the skills and experiences garnered from my study abroad participation, I would not currently be a successful volunteer in Morocco, and I certainly would not be the same person that I am today.

I am extremely grateful to Dr. Eimad Houry for mentoring me throughout my four years of undergraduate study at Mercer University and for encouraging me to take advantage of every opportunity to study abroad that I encountered. I am also grateful to my parents, who graciously funded my participation in these programs and who have always supported my wanderlust, then and now. And I want to make special mention of Dr. Anwah Nagia, the visionary behind the District Six Museum and the Palestine Museum and Human Rights Center in Cape Town, South Africa, who passed away in 2020 during the COVID-19 pandemic; *ʾinnā li-llāhi wa-ʾinnā ʾilayhi rājiʿūn.**

Spring Break in Dubai, March 2017

The semester during which I participated in the faculty-led Spring Break in Dubai was the same semester in which I was taking a separate class on Middle East Politics, and in many respects, the trip was an extension of the coursework. Not only was the professor the same for the class and the preparatory colloquium on Dubai, but I was also eagerly looking forward to directly applying the information we had studied in the classroom to a Middle Eastern context. The program in Dubai as its name suggests, was a brief, ten-day trip arranged and guided by a university professor for cultural exposure in and promoting awareness of the societies of the Middle East.

Dubai is not a country; rather, it is one of the seven emirates that compose a federation called the United Arab Emirates (UAE). Its development boom is immediately visible upon arrival in Dubai, which is home to several of the world's most iconic architectural landmarks. I had the opportunity to visit many of these spectacles during the trip, including the Burj Khalifa (the tallest building in the world), the artificial islands that make up the Palm Jumeirah, the Jumeirah Beach Hotel (shaped like a massive sail), and the famous luxury hotel Burj Al Arab. Nevertheless, however grand and marvelous these buildings—and the rest of Dubai's skyline—may be, they are not as interesting as the stories and lives of the people who live there. One of the few interactions our group had with a

* "Verily, we belong to God, and verily to him we shall return."

local Emirati was one of the most memorable and poignant episodes of the entire trip, in my recollection. During our visit to the Sheikh Al Maktoum Center for Cultural Understanding, I found myself in conversation with one of the center's organizers, who recounted his personal story of growing up in Dubai. The emirate of his childhood was nothing like the modern city it is today, and he explained the poverty and underdevelopment that characterized Dubai before the discovery of oil in the Persian Gulf. His favorite memory as a child was playing football in a barren field and competing with his friends for the privilege of drinking Coca-Cola, an imported luxury at the time. He was simultaneously very proud of what his country had become while also lamenting that something—he very well may have said "authenticity"—was lost in the transition. His nostalgia deeply affected me.

The Al Maktoum Center, as a component of its "Open Doors, Open Minds" program, offers visits to the Jumeirah Mosque along with a presentation of basic Islamic beliefs and rituals. In the six years since I participated in the Spring Break in Dubai program, I have visited more than a dozen Muslim-majority countries, and I currently live and work in one. I am thoroughly accustomed to mosques now, but the visit to the Jumeirah Mosque was the first time I had ever entered one. In reading my travel journals from that period today, I realize I had forgotten how excited I was to enter a mosque for the first time in my life. My initial reactions to its design and to how Muslims utilize the space, to say nothing of the rituals, prostrations, and synchronization of Islamic prayers, were completely new to me. I wrote that I was bewildered by the *adhan*—the call that precedes the five daily Islamic prayers—which today is completely normal to me. Tangibly, Spring Break in Dubai was my first real exposure to Islam.

Ten days is simply not enough time for an immersive experience, but it is enough for an introduction, which was the stated goal of the program. It succeeded in meeting that objective, and I am thankful to have participated in it. What the UAE left with me was a set of new ideas and impressions about what the Middle East is, or can be. It is a place of rapid change and development—as evidenced by the story of my interlocutor at the Al Maktoum Center—with a dynamic and predominantly young population capable of creating marvels like the Burj Khalifa and ambitious projects like Masdar City. And here I will share my strongest memory of Dubai: when I look back, the image of construction cranes busily whirling around always comes to mind. Indeed, the UAE is said to be home to a quarter of all of the world's functioning cranes, and in Dubai, they are emblazoned with the stark logos of Emaar and DAMAC, Emirati companies that are building a "New Middle East." That impression of dynamism and rapid change has been the foundation for my interactions with the Middle East ever since.

Mercer on Mission in Georgia, June to July 2017

I participated in the Mercer on Mission program in the country of Georgia, where we worked with two community partners—the World Association of Georgian Muslims and the International Humanitarian Charity Association "BETELLI." The fact that I stayed in an Islamic boarding school and was immersed in an Islamic community may come as a surprise to those familiar with Georgia, which claims to be one of the oldest formally Christian nations on earth, in competition with Armenia and Ethiopia. Georgia is both an ancient nation, with an unbroken national narrative dating back to the tenth century, and a relatively new nation, having achieved political independence as a modern state only in 1991 with the collapse of the Soviet Union. Throughout its long history, Georgia has enjoyed periods of independence interspersed with foreign domination, having been subject to Islamic rule under the Ottoman and Safavid Empires before being conquered by the Russian Empire in the eighteenth century. In the nationalist telling of Georgia's history, despite the frequent lapse of sovereignty, the "Georgian nation" has been sustained since its inception by its devotion to the Georgian Orthodox Church; thus, in the nationalist imagination, to belong to the "Georgian nation" means to belong to the Georgian Orthodox Church, in addition to speaking the unique Georgian language.

It was first in Georgia that I began to seriously grapple with questions of identity and nationalism through the analysis of two distinct yet related questions. First, is Georgia a European country, or, phrased differently, what does it mean to be European? Second, what does it mean to be Georgian? I still do not have answers to these questions—neither do Europeans and Georgians themselves, for that matter—but our attempt to understand them in Georgia has strongly influenced my worldview, my academic interests, and the way I now perceive similar discourse in other contexts.

Georgian nationalists deny that the Muslim population is Georgian, but the Muslims in Adjara and the rest of Georgia insist that they are. They speak the Georgian language, have lived there for several generations, and share nearly identical food and cuisine with the rest of the country. In all other respects besides religion, they are just like every other Georgian. Their version of Georgian identity is simply not conditioned on belonging to the Georgian Orthodox Church.

In addition to raising key questions about nationalism and identity, Georgia also gave me my first interaction with interfaith dialogue and cross-cultural communication. A key player in this opening was our host, Malkhaz Songulashvili, who heads the International Humanitarian Charity Association "BETELLI" and is also the Metropolitan Bishop of Tbilisi for the Evangelical-Baptist Church of Georgia. As a Georgian who does not belong to the Orthodox Church, he and his community are subject to the same nationalist pressures that affect Muslim Georgians in Adjara, so Songulashvili is closely connected with activists from other marginalized communities, including the Muslim, non-Orthodox Christian, and

LGBTQ+ communities, to advocate for an expanded view of Georgian identity. A key component of his project is the construction of the Peace Cathedral in Tbilisi, a unique religious building that will function simultaneously as a church, a mosque, and a synagogue. Contributing manpower to construct this cathedral was a small secondary project during our limited time in Tbilisi, but I remain proud to have been involved in this noble venture.

If the mosques in Dubai and Abu Dhabi were foreign to me, by the end of my time in Georgia, I was fully acquainted with their inner workings and diverse functions after living and working as an English tutor in an Islamic boarding school during the summer of 2017. One of my objectives was to integrate with my students as much as possible, and to do so, I went with them to the mosque attached to the school five times a day, waking up before dawn for the Fajr prayer and going with them after dark to complete the Isha prayer, with three more throughout the day. I learned how to properly complete *wudu*—ritual washing— before each prayer, memorized the first chapter of the Quran, and finally grew comfortable with the *adhan* that had so startled me in the UAE. Defying the expectations of my students, however, I never did convert to Islam, although before my departure they gifted me a prayer rug, a copy of the Quran, and a *taqiyya*—an Islamic skullcap. I was only in Georgia for a month, yet my experiences there left a lasting impression on me and altered my academic interests. I remained an international affairs major with key interests in the Middle East and North Africa region (MENA), but it is not difficult to apply the lessons about narrative, discourse, nationalism, and identity that I learned in Georgia to other countries in the Middle East, especially in deeply sectarian environments like Lebanon or Iraq. Around this time, I also decided to formally commit to pursuing a major in religion as well; my experiences in Georgia played no small part in that addition. To this day I remain committed to interfaith dialogue and have been involved in several extracurricular activities on campus to pursue such a dialogue: I am a founding member of Mercer BEARS (Bears Engaged Across Religions), and I am actively working to promote cross-cultural communication through my work with the Peace Corps in Morocco. Since graduating from Mercer University, I have found an intellectual home in postcolonial studies, which I intend to pursue at the graduate level shortly; this is a field where narratives around nationalism and identity are critically important.

Gateway KSA, February to March 2018

During my participation in the Kingdom of Saudi Arabia's "Gateway KSA" pilot program in the spring of 2018, I had the privilege of meeting His Royal Highness Prince Turki bin Faisal Al Saud in his home in Riyadh, Saudi Arabia, where he told me that Americans often make harsh judgments about Arab countries because of the vast geographical and cultural distance between the United States and the Arab world. Arab policymakers do not have the same physical or cultural separation from the region that Americans have. Rather, they must make immediate choices for immediate problems to obtain immediate results. I often think about what he said to me, especially when trying to understand the objectives and motivations of key decision-makers in the Middle East and what tools are available for them to achieve said objectives.

Gateway KSA is a program sponsored by the King Faisal Center for Research and Islamic Studies that is similar to the faculty-led Spring Break in Dubai program. Program participants are invited to a nine-day guided tour of Saudi Arabia and invited to attend seminars with key policymakers, authorities, and academics from Saudi universities. The program was launched in 2018 as part of a broader initiative by the Saudi government to promote the launch of their new tourist visa and to showcase the increasing openness of the kingdom to foreigners. We were accompanied and frequently interviewed by a news crew from the Rotana Group, a popular telecommunications company in Saudi Arabia that eventually produced a documentary about our experiences.

The design of Gateway KSA's program was structured in such a way that its participants would leave the country with a full understanding of the Saudi national narrative; I was already putting my experiences with identity construction in Georgia to good use in analyzing what we were witnessing in Saudi Arabia. The trip began in Riyadh with a tour of Masmak Fortress, the most important historical landmark in the city, where Ibn Saud won an important battle in 1902 and established the Third Saudi State, the modern Kingdom of Saudi Arabia. Then we were taken just outside of Riyadh to the nearby town of Diriyah, which was the capital of the First Saudi State and ancestral home of the Al Saud ruling dynasty. For good measure, we were subsequently taken to the National Museum of Saudi Arabia, and eventually, Gateway KSA took us to Dammam on the Gulf coast to see for ourselves the second pillar of the Saudi state: Dammam No. 7, the first oil well in Saudi Arabia, which began production in 1938, and the headquarters of Aramco, the state-owned oil company.

Gateway KSA was similar to Spring Break in Dubai in that the limited period spent in Saudi Arabia—only nine days— provided little more than an introduction to the country, its culture, and its people. However, given the explicit state backing for the program, we were able to meet with a large variety of key figures and academics in Saudi Arabia. Prince Turki bin Faisal was by far the most influential person we met, and we discussed a large array of topics with him, ranging from the ongoing war in Yemen to the role of Saudi Arabia in the "New Middle East." We also met with the governor of Eastern Province, Saud bin Nayef Al Saud, who presides over the heartland of the Saudi oil economy. We attended a seminar at Effat University, a women's university in Jeddah, where we discussed the issue of women's rights in Saudi Arabia and the achievements of an indigenous Saudi feminist movement. And at King Abdullah

University of Science and Technology (KAUST), the first coeducational university in Saudi Arabia, both male and female students shared their research projects with much enthusiasm and pride. Finally, back in Riyadh, we took part in discussions with security analysts who unexpectedly described the need for Saudi Arabia to adopt policies that favor the expansion of human security—an approach that elevates the importance of universal human rights—across the Middle East.

I learned a great deal about Saudi Arabia from my participation with Gateway KSA, although I am fully aware that the information and narratives that we were provided had the official sanction of the Saudi state. Nonetheless, my experience there has proven valuable in my understanding of how Saudi Arabia perceives itself in the world and consequently how it acts and behaves. I left Saudi Arabia with an overall impression not unlike that of Dubai: it is a society in a state of transition, aware of its past and enthusiastic about its future, eager to build a new Saudi Arabia and achieve Mohammed bin Salman's Vision 2030, and ready to be an active player in the "New Middle East."

Study Abroad in Lebanon, June to August 2018

The Emaar and DAMAC cranes that I had left behind in the UAE in March 2017 appeared before me once again upon my arrival in Beirut, Lebanon, in June 2018. Almost thirty years after the end of the Lebanese Civil War (1975–1990), the city of Beirut and much of Lebanon remain deeply scarred and are still struggling to repair and rebuild not only infrastructure but also the deeply fractured Lebanese society. Capital and investment injected from the Persian Gulf states like the UAE and Saudi Arabia can help to overcome the first challenge; only the Lebanese themselves can overcome the second.

I believe it is possible to teach a course on Middle East politics by only teaching the history of Lebanon. Almost every geopolitical rivalry within the Middle East since decolonization has a fault line running through Lebanon, one of the most diverse sectarian states in the region. The territory of modern-day Lebanon was occupied by France in 1920 as a part of the much wider French mandate in Syria after the partition of the Ottoman Empire. In 1923, the French split their mandate into two new states by dividing Lebanon from the rest of Syria; the French goal was the creation of an independent Christian state in the Middle East, which France predicted would remain a loyal ally of the West. However, at the time of the division, Lebanese Christians only formed roughly half of the population, while the other half was predominantly Muslim with a Druze minority. Only the animosity between Sunni and Shia Muslims prevented a unified opposition and gave the Christians a plurality in national politics.

I was in Lebanon from June to August 2018 as a participant in the Arabic Language and Culture Program offered by the Center for Arab and Middle Eastern Studies (CAMES) at the American University in Beirut (AUB). This program is an extensive Arabic-language summer course offered to applicants from around the world, and after my previous interactions with the Middle East in the UAE and Saudi Arabia and about a year of independent study, I was excited and eager to finally study the Arabic language in a formal setting. At the time, no such opportunities existed at Mercer, so learning the language would have been impossible without the opportunity to study abroad. Furthermore, while my faculty advisor encouraged me to apply to CAMES, my application and eventual involvement were completely independent of Mercer University and do not appear on my academic transcript.

When I arrived at AUB, I took a placement exam to gauge my experience with the Arabic language and was ultimately placed in the beginner's intermediate class. The two instructors represented the diversity of Lebanese society—one was a Christian and the other was a Shia Muslim—while the class tutor paired with us was a Shia Muslim. My fellow classmates and I signed a pledge promising to commit ourselves to using Arabic as fully as possible in all classes and activities and with all participants, including each other, making the program truly an immersive experience. This fact, combined with the necessity of learning Arabic to communicate with locals off-campus, greatly enhanced the experience, and I found myself picking up the language much quicker than I initially expected.

The CAMES program was the first study abroad program in which I participated that was wholly unguided. Aside from the highly structured time in the classroom—about eight hours a day—I was there in Beirut in a fully individual capacity. For the first time abroad, I could travel freely and choose how I would spend my free time and engage with Lebanese society and culture. At first, this was very intimidating, especially since I was still new to the language, but over time I gained more confidence and began to arrange trips for myself further from AUB's campus into Beirut and even outside of Beirut into the rest of Lebanon. I had the opportunity to travel as far north as Jounieh and Byblos, as far south as Sidon, and even visited Deir El Qamar and Beit ed-Dine in the interior. This would not have been possible without my prior experience in the UAE, Georgia, and Saudi Arabia, all of which contributed to my confidence in navigating abroad.

In addition to my studies in Arabic, while at AUB I also volunteered with the Kayany Foundation, a group that provides humanitarian aid to Syrian refugees living in Lebanon; more than 1.5 million refugees from Syria lived in Lebanon during my time in Beirut. On the weekends, I worked with young children, both male and female, at a refugee camp near the city of Zahlé, where I organized recreational and youth development activities similar to my current work with the Peace Corps in Morocco. My interactions with Syrian refugees in Lebanon, and especially their children, were deeply sobering. My interest in the Middle East, its geopolitics, and its conflicts could no longer be simply academic, and I came away from this experience deeply aware of the real-life consequences for ordinary people who suffer needlessly as a result of decisions made in faraway capitals to secure vaguely defined national objectives.

This realization was further enhanced by my decision to visit the Sabra and Shatila refugee camps toward the end of my time in Lebanon after I had gained enough skill and confidence in Arabic to communicate effectively. Sabra and Shatila were the sites of terrible massacres of civilian refugees between September 16 and 18, 1982. Israeli soldiers had complete control of the camps from the exterior and allowed their Christian Lebanese allies from the Lebanese forces to enter the camps and murder more than three thousand Palestinians with impunity. This was only weeks after the Palenstine Liberation Organization had disarmed Lebanon and transferred its leadership and fighters to Tunisia in August 1982 under the auspices of the American Marines then deployed in Lebanon; all of the victims in Sabra and Shatila were therefore unarmed civilians. The massacres rank among the greatest tragedies of the Lebanese Civil War and the Arab-Israeli conflict as a whole, yet the camps remain in operation today and are still home to Palestinian refugees unable to return to their homeland after being displaced in 1948 and 1967. Visiting the camps and engaging with their residents—"survivors" is perhaps more apt—was an emotional and haunting experience.

My poignant exposure to Palestinians in Lebanon would soon be bolstered by direct experiences with the Israeli occupation in Palestine itself. After leaving Lebanon, I had about two weeks before I needed to arrive in Morocco for my next study abroad opportunity, so rather than return to the United States briefly, I chose to remain in the Middle East. I consider these travel experiences a component of my study abroad in Lebanon; after all, it was only because I participated in CAMES that I was able to communicate effectively and arrange my travels. I left Lebanon for a short stay in Kuwait before proceeding to Jordan, and after a few days exploring Jordan—Amman, Jerash, Ajloun, Madaba, and Petra—I crossed the land border into Palestine. I stayed in Jerusalem and from there made several trips to the outlying areas of the West Bank, including Ramallah and Bethlehem. I witnessed firsthand various facets of the ongoing Israeli occupation—discriminatory treatment, military checkpoints, arbitrary road closures—and was deeply shocked at the massive apartheid wall that cuts through the Palestinian landscape. I visited the Palestinians at the Aida Camp who were made refugees in their land, and I observed for myself the proliferating Israeli settlements encroaching on Palestinian land. I left via Tel Aviv thoroughly disgusted by the situation and relieved to be able to escape, but the Palestinians in the West Bank and Gaza do not have that privilege.

Overall, my participation with CAMES and the American University in Beirut was a deeply transformative experience, more so than any of my prior study abroad opportunities. I entered the program as a complete novice in speaking the Arabic language, but after three months I was able to communicate effectively and interact with Arabic speakers not only in Lebanon but also in Kuwait, Jordan, and Palestine. This had long been an important academic objective for me, yet I learned in Lebanon that my engagement with the Middle East could no longer be simply academic. My fuller understanding of Lebanese history, my interactions with Syrian and Palestinian refugees, and my subsequent harrowing experiences in Palestine itself put me on a path toward deeper engagement with the Arab-Israeli conflict that would eventually come to dominate my academic and professional commitments.

Study Abroad in Morocco, August to December 2018

After departing from Palestine, I spent several days in Istanbul, Türkiye, before continuing onward to Morocco, my final destination for the fall 2018 semester starting in August. Unlike the CAMES program in Lebanon, my semester abroad at Al Akhawayn University in Ifrane, Morocco, was organized through an exchange program offered by Mercer University; therefore, it took place during the normal academic year (as opposed to the summer program in Lebanon) so my credits from Al Akhawayn appear on my Mercer transcript. Upon arrival, I was surprised to discover that the Arabic I had used to communicate in Lebanon, Jordan, and Palestine was an entirely different dialect from Moroccan Arabic, or Darija. I could communicate effectively in Modern Standard Arabic and Lebanese Arabic, but outside of the classroom at Al Akhawayn everyone spoke to me in Darija, which I could not understand at the time.

I was simultaneously studying French as well, having already completed two semesters of the language at Mercer (I would eventually complete a minor in French). While I struggled in Arabic class, my French improved tremendously, especially since I was using it for daily communication off campus, where, since I couldn't understand Darija, most people spoke to me in French. For the duration of my studies at Al Akhawayn, Morocco seemed to me to be primarily a francophone country, rather than an Arabic-speaking one. I was surprised to learn that French is not technically the official language of Morocco, yet it remains the language of business and everyday administration for most of the country. Significantly, French is also the language of the Moroccan elite.

A third major topic of study I pursued while attending Al Akhawayn was furthering my interest in Islam. I took two relevant courses: Introduction to Islamic Law and Jurisprudence, and Introduction to the Study of Islamic Civilization. No comparable courses on these subjects were yet available at Mercer, so once again the option to study abroad was the only way to expand my familiarity with Islamic studies during my undergraduate career. Both classes were composed of foreign exchange students like me and local students, and my interactions with Moroccan students in this context taught me insightful lessons about how Moroccans perceive and practice Islam. In my opinion, they contributed just as much to my education as my professors.

A final element worth reflecting upon during my semester abroad in Morocco is the numerous opportunities I had to travel. Building upon my prior experiences in the Middle East, I was finally comfortable enough to take advantage of every opportunity to experience the diverse locales and cultures of Morocco; I pledged not to spend a single weekend on-campus at Al Akhawayn if I could avoid it. I quickly became acquainted with the buses, trains, and *grands taxis* to travel extensively, venturing from Tanger, Tetouan, and Chefchaouen in the north to Marrakech, Ouarzazate, Essaouira, and Dakhla in the south. I even managed to find myself in Mauritania, where I ventured deep into the Sahara Desert from Nouakchott to Chinguetti, in addition to weekend trips to Spain and France. Upon the completion of the semester in December 2018, I returned to the United States in a roundabout way, hopping across the Mediterranean and spending several days each in Italy, Tunisia, and Egypt before finally heading home in early January 2019.

My semester abroad at Al Akhawayn University in Morocco was the longest single study abroad experience I participated in during my undergraduate studies, and it also contributed the most to my academic development, with unique opportunities to study Arabic and several topics in the field of Islamic studies in addition to furthering my studies of French. However, in hindsight, I believe my French skills improved much more than my skills in Arabic, simply because I needed to develop French (or Darija, which was not an option) to communicate successfully, and I struggled with the different pedagogy in the Arabic department. The deep impact left on me by my time in Morocco should be evidenced by the fact that I decided to return in 2022 to dedicate at least two years of my life (and potentially more) to serving in Morocco with the US Peace Corps. Put simply, I found a second home.

Internship in South Africa, May to August 2019

There is an expression in Moroccan Arabic that says "*Fīhā ḥayr,*" meaning, "There is good in it." It is usually used for situations that did not turn out as expected but ultimately worked out for the best. I experienced the sentiment behind this expression during my internship in Cape Town, South Africa, in the summer of 2019. When I boarded the plane for Cape Town, I was expecting to arrive in South Africa and work as an intern at the Iziko South African Museum, but when I disembarked, I was surprised to learn that the museum recently changed management and was longer seeking an intern. This situation worked out for the best in the end, however, as I managed to find a similar opportunity at the Palestine Museum and Human Rights Center.

The Palestine Museum is the brainchild of Dr. Anwah Nagia, a well-known and respected anti-apartheid activist who had previously contributed to the foundation of the District Six Museum, also in Cape Town. For South Africans like Dr. Nagia, it is difficult not to describe the ongoing situation in Palestine as a system of apartheid comparable to the system that existed in South Africa until 1994. The Palestine Museum and Human Rights Center is an effort to document the tragedy of Palestinian dispossession from Israel during the 1948 Nakba and from the West Bank and Gaza Strip during the 1967 Six-Day War while also bearing witness to the decades-long Palestinian struggle for justice and recognition in their ancestral lands.

Given my continued academic interest in national narratives, nationalism, and the processes of identity formation, along with my extensive background in the Middle East and especially in the Arab-Israeli conflict, the internship was an ideal role for me to fill. The museum at the time was still under construction, and my primary project was to curate a proposed exhibit showcasing the Palestinian villages that were depopulated and destroyed during the establishment of the State of Israel in 1948. The work was relatively straightforward since Palestinian civil society and activist groups have been doing research in this area for several decades. The major tasks at hand were to comb through information from both English and Arabic sources, authenticate claims from government sources with academic studies drawing from eyewitness testimonials and population data from British and Ottoman records, cross-reference site locations and names, resolve discrepancies and standardize the transliteration of place-names, and finally decide on the most appropriate way to present the data in the museum itself. Dr. Nagia decided on a massive map that would occupy most of the floor space on the ground level of the museum, with each destroyed village represented by a special tile with the name, population, and date of destruction. I then spent several weeks preparing 418 such tiles, one for every Palestinian village destroyed by Israel in 1948.

My internship at the Palestine Museum and Human Rights Center in Cape Town, South Africa, was the culmination of my study abroad experiences while I was an undergraduate student at Mercer University. It was the time and the place where all of my prior experiences in Georgia and the Middle East seemed to come together to complete a work project that was not only personally fulfilling but also deeply connected to my academic and career interests. I used my background in Arabic and firsthand knowledge of the Arab-Israeli conflict to contribute to meaningful change and to educate the general public in Cape Town. Using the skills I developed in South Africa, I became an advocate for the Palestinian cause upon my return to Mercer for my senior year, where I established a chapter for Students for Justice in Palestine (SJP). One might even say that in Cape Town *I found my calling*.

Concluding Notes

In the above narratives, I have attempted to capture moments and experiences from my participation in six study abroad programs and narrate their tangible and intangible effects on my development. I became proficient in two foreign languages, French and Arabic, as a result of studying abroad, and the opportunity to study Arabic was only available by going abroad. I spent extensive time immersed in Arabic and Islamic communities and am now quite comfortable in these environments; reading my initial reflections on my first interactions with Islam in Dubai now makes me chuckle. I am successfully able to engage in cross-cultural communication and work and live long-term in a foreign context. I became a committed supporter of the cause of justice in Palestine. My earliest experiences with nationalism and identity formation in Georgia were deepened with continued interactions in Lebanon, Palestine, Morocco, and South Africa, so much so that I now seek to pursue these subjects at the graduate level in the field of postcolonial studies upon completion of my service with the Peace Corps in Morocco. More intangibly, I am a product of hundreds of individual interactions with people from around the world, not just local people in the Middle East but also a whole network of other exchange students that I met at AUB and Al Akhawayn University.

Upon my return to the United States, I found myself in a unique position on Mercer's campus and in the wider community as a result of my experiences abroad, and I was able to leverage those experiences in many areas of my academic and professional life. Most immediately, my involvement on campus changed as I became involved in areas and extracurricular activities where I could use and demonstrate my newfound skills and knowledge. In addition to my involvement with Mercer SJP and Mercer BEARS, I also became an active participant with the National Council for US-Arab Relations through its Model Arab League Program, in which I headed my university's delegation to regional and national conferences on several occasions and even served as a national committee chairman from 2018 to 2019. In partnership with my faculty advisor, I worked as a teaching assistant for two semesters in a newly developed class on Arabic language and culture and for a semester in a class on Middle East politics. Finally, my two senior theses—one on Martin Buber's interpretation of and role in Zionist thought and the other on Islamist and leftist political alliances in the Middle East—were undoubtedly informed and enriched by my diverse background in the Middle East and North Africa. I graduated from Mercer viewed by many of my peers as a budding authority on the region, and I was eager to return as soon as possible. I highlighted my study abroad experiences in my application and was rapidly accepted to serve with the Peace Corps in Morocco. I am now near the midpoint of my two-year service, and I am incredibly proud of my current work to build youth skills and to develop increased understanding between the Moroccan and American public. I find my service quite fulfilling and one of the best outcomes to emerge from my study abroad experiences at Mercer University.

My advice for students seeking study abroad opportunities is threefold.

- First, one should start considering what study abroad opportunities are available at prospective universities before making the final commitment to attend one or the other. In my opinion, study abroad programs are just as important as academic opportunities, school facilities, housing, cost-of-living considerations, extracurricular activities, and the like, and such programs definitely should not be overlooked or relegated to secondary importance. As I related in my introduction, the opportunities for study abroad available at Mercer were a key factor in my decision to attend this particular university.

- Second, one should develop a close relationship with one's faculty advisor and communicate the desire to study abroad as early as possible. Not only was my faculty advisor the responsible professor for two of my study abroad experiences—Spring

Break in Dubai and Mercer on Mission in Georgia— he was instrumental in seeking other opportunities for me as well, especially Gateway KSA and my semester abroad at AUB in Lebanon. Nor can I overlook his involvement in ensuring that my participation in these programs contributed to my academic plan and helped me leverage these experiences academically and professionally when I returned to campus.

- Finally, one should not feel that one's major is a limiting factor in deciding to study abroad. As an international affairs major, I can admit that my particular major is more obviously conducive to studying abroad than most, yet throughout my undergraduate studies I encountered dozens of other participants who were not international affairs majors. For example, one of my close friends that I met while studying abroad at Al Akhawayn University was a German exchange student who was pursuing a degree in business management. Regardless of one's major, the challenges of studying abroad and the skills resulting from meeting them—such as intercultural competency, personal resiliency, and foreign language development—are interdisciplinary; they can be leveraged and applied in almost every career path. Furthermore, at a university like Mercer, where a multitude of different study abroad opportunities exists, there is sure to be a program that can be incorporated into any academic major.

When I reflect on my four years at Mercer University from 2016 to 2020, studying abroad towers over all other experiences that I had on campus in terms of personal impact and academic and career importance. In retrospect, I don't think there is anything about studying abroad that I would change. On the contrary, I cannot emphasize enough the unique opportunities offered by study abroad programs for personal growth and global awareness, and I strongly encourage every student to take advantage of them.

NEW KNOWLEDGE AND NEW PERSPECTIVES

19

UNDERSTANDING AMID COMPLEXITY

Alec M. Campbell

International Affairs
Class of 2022

"He who wants to travel far spares his mount."
—French Proverb

In March 2022, I had the opportunity to join a group of undergraduate Mercer University students on a rigorous eleven-day Spring Break Israel study abroad program. This was a life-changing experience that allowed me to learn more about diverse and fascinating cultures, and to critically examine the health and human rights challenges that exist among the vast communities inhabiting the region. This program was designed to delve into the complex intersection of health issues and human rights within Israeli society, and how such challenges affect physical, mental, emotional, and spiritual health on the individual level. The course included classroom lectures, site visits to healthcare facilities and NGOs, and multiple meetings with local experts and community members. As I reflect on my study abroad experience two years later, I am still in awe of the profound impact my time in Israel has had on my understanding of health and human rights, intercultural awareness, and practical skills.

Studying abroad has always held a special allure for me. The opportunity to immerse myself in a different culture, surround myself with a new language, and gain a deeper understanding of global issues was something I had longed for. I was motivated to participate in this particular study abroad program for several reasons. First, I wanted to learn more about the conflict surrounding Israel and Palestine. As a then international affairs student, I was fascinated by this region, and I wanted to gain a better understanding of the history and politics of the conflict. I wanted to explore what effect the conflict was having on the physical and mental health of ordinary citizens. Second, I wanted to learn about the health and human rights challenges, particularly those related to the accessibility of healthcare. Third, there were certainly some nonacademic reasons that attracted me to the program. The opportunity to explore the many ancient and sacred holy sites such as the Al-Aqsa Mosque, the Western Wall, the Masada, and the Church of the Holy Sepulcher convinced me to spend spring break of my senior year in Israel. This trip was the perfect opportunity to observe and study how the many social, economic, political, and cultural challenges Israelis and Palestinians face can affect their overall health.

Israeli society is multiethnic and multireligious. It hosts diverse ethnolinguistic and religious groups including Jews from diverse cultural backgrounds and Arabs of diverse religious persuasions as well as people of Bedouin and Druze ethnicity. The region's geography is marked by religious and cultural sites of significance to Judaism, Christianity, and Islam, making these places both a focal point of global attention as well as an embodiment of the beautiful cultural tapestry that represents Israel and Palestine. Despite the unique blending of customs I witnessed while I was there, Israel and Palestine have a long and turbulent history characterized by conflicting territorial claims, ethnic tensions, and competing narratives.

The political landscape in Israel and Palestine is complex, with opposing national identities and aspirations. The Israeli-Palestinian conflict has been a source of protracted violence and diplomatic disputes. Studying the intersections between culture, religion, politics, geography, and health in such an eclectic society provided an enriching learning experience.

Our Mercer group spent its first days in the cosmopolitan city of Tel Aviv. The city was saturated with diversity, with people of all faiths and backgrounds intermingling in the many picturesque public spaces. This intermingling was especially distinct in the neighborhood of Jaffa, a bustling quarter on the beach, which we had the chance to explore. On our way to Haifa, we visited the Bible college in Netanya, where we engaged in a constructive dialogue and gained more knowledge on how the college, which admits Jewish, Arab, and Christian students, functions daily. We wanted to understand the impact of such multiethnic programs on the peace and reconciliation work in the region.

As we continued our journey, we made a brief stop at the Hadrianic Aqueduct of Caesarea. Known as King Herod's Aqueduct, it is one of Israel's most famous archaeological sites. At the University of Haifa, we attended a lecture led by professors and staff at the School of Public Health, where we gained greater insight into the demographics of the school, how the region was recovering from the 2020 COVID-19 pandemic, recent health trends in the country, and the Israeli healthcare system. We learned that shortly after our arrival Israel reported its first polio case in years, much to the alarm of local health officials. This news proved that more must be done to educate and reassure the local communities, especially traditional ones, that vaccines are essential to prevention efforts. Furthermore, I learned that the Israeli government recognizes healthcare as a human right. Therefore, all Israeli nationals have access to a well-maintained state-run healthcare system. Despite this principle being enshrined, there was still a small percentage of communities that remained uninsured or unable to fully access healthcare in the country. These included, but were not limited to, people with disabilities and refugees. While the Palestinian Authority is responsible for the healthcare needs of Palestinians, the conflict creates major obstacles to maintaining well-functioning health infrastructure in the Palestinian territories.

Near the end of our trip, we traveled to Be'er Sheva, located south of Jerusalem. This community has a large population of Ethiopian Jews and their descendants, which provided us with a unique perspective on how the experience of being Jewish and Israeli citizens can change if one has brown or black skin. We learned that Ethiopian Jews in Israel often have faced, and continue to face, racial discrimination, which affects their political, social, and economic mobility in Israeli society. Likewise, this has consequences for their general health as access to healthcare becomes more challenging due to economic barriers and lack of healthcare facilities in the community. Hearing these perspectives was eye-opening.

One of the most tangible benefits of studying health and human rights in Israel was the significant deepening of my understanding of these complex issues. This firsthand exposure to healthcare facilities and direct insight from experts and citizens allowed me to witness the challenges faced by healthcare professionals, patients, and marginalized communities. Conversations with healthcare providers and community members provided valuable insights into the disparities in healthcare access and their impact on the mental and physical well-being of individuals.

Discussions about the limited access to healthcare for marginalized communities—mainly the Jews of Ethiopian descent, Palestinians, refugees, and the disabled—reminded us that even in a country where health is a human right, there are still members of society who may not get what they need. Fortunately, we were able to gain a closer insight into the advocacy efforts that shed light on the resilience of civil society organizations working tirelessly to address these challenges. One such organization is the Shalva National Center in Jerusalem, which dedicates its services to children with disabilities. Witnessing the dedication of individuals and organizations striving to uphold human rights in the face of adversity left a lasting impression on me. This experience significantly enriched my understanding of the intricate interplay between the political and civil society spheres in an inequitable country like Israel.

Studying health in the context of Israeli society profoundly affected my intercultural understanding and global consciousness. Exposure to diverse viewpoints and experiences challenged my preconceived notions and stereotypes. Engaging in conversations with Palestinians, Israelis, and international peers gave me a multifaceted understanding of the complexities of the conflict, particularly as it relates to health.

Witnessing the daily lives of individuals living amidst a backdrop of geopolitical tension fostered empathy and a deep appreciation for the resilience of the human spirit. *I came to recognize that the narratives and experiences of the people and communities of Israel and Palestine were more nuanced than I had previously understood. This realization has been instrumental in shaping my approach to global issues, emphasizing the importance of dialogue, empathy, and open-mindedness when addressing complex health-related challenges worldwide.*

My study abroad experience in Israel also shaped specific practical skills that I have continued to use since graduating. First and foremost, it strengthened my research and critical thinking abilities. Analyzing the multifaceted aspects of health and human rights in such a brief time required rigorous research, a critical assessment of sources, and the ability to synthesize complex information—a skillset that has been indispensable in my postgraduate work with NGOs and research institutions.

Furthermore, the experience honed my adaptability and resilience. Exploring a region fraught with political tension taught me to navigate uncertain situations with composure, an open mind, and a great deal of empathy. These skills have proven valuable in both my personal and professional life, helping me approach challenges with a positive mindset and a solution-oriented approach. To maximize the impact of study abroad on the next generation, I would offer the following tips to prospective students:

- Embrace discomfort and take a chance: Engaging with different cultures and confronting complex issues may be uncomfortable, but it is in these moments that the most profound growth occurs. Be open to new experiences and perspectives. And if you see an opportunity that is calling to you, take it.
- Engage with the local community: Interact with locals, make an effort to at least learn one word or phrase in their native tongue, and immerse yourself in the culture. These connections can provide insights and experiences that go far beyond the classroom.
- Seek diverse perspectives: Engage in conversations with people from various backgrounds, including locals, fellow students, and experts in the field. This will broaden your understanding and foster empathy. Turn to your friends and classmates for help and clarity, as their perspectives will be just as enriching.
- Reflect and document: Keep a journal or blog to document your experiences and reflections. This can help you process your thoughts, solidify your learning, and share your journey with others. Thankfully, Dr. Obidoa had journals and an itinerary made for us, which was filled in just the first few days we were there.
- Stay hydrated, prepared, and comfortable: Pack a water bottle and drink plenty of water for those long journeys, lectures, and flights. Your brain will thank you. Also, be sure to bring a portable first-aid kit. You don't want to be caught empty-handed with a headache, blisters, or an upset stomach. Finally, bring some comfortable nonslip shoes for wherever your journey takes you.

20

WE ARE MORE SIMILAR THAN WE ARE DIFFERENT: DEEP LEARNING ON SELF, LIFE, AND THE WORLD

Alyssa Fortner

International Affairs and Global Development Studies
Class of 2020

"If you are traveling towards the East, you will inevitably move away from the West."
—Japanese Proverb

Having grown up as a multiracial girl in a small, homogenous Georgia town with a population of about three thousand people—a microcosm of the stereotypical ideas around Southern, conservative towns—I declared my first major in international affairs at eighteen without ever having left the American South. When I look back on this decision, I know it directly stems from the limited opportunities I had to expand my consciousness and experiences beyond a small, isolated environment. I was convinced that where I was would not be the only place, people, and perspectives I would ever know and understand, and my first step in this journey took me to Mercer University. Without Mercer's study abroad programs, I would never have had a meaningful opportunity to grow beyond my upbringing.

I was uncertain of my ultimate career goal, but I knew I wanted my studies to encompass as many global issues and experiences as possible. I was looking to merge my own valuable, lived experiences with new knowledge and authentic immersions to hopefully develop a well-rounded global consciousness. In this spirit, I pursued a double major in international affairs and global development studies with a minor in anthropology during my four years at Mercer. Through this journey, I was exposed to new perspectives, diverse life experiences, cultures, both domestic and international politics and policies, and more, while also having the opportunity to travel abroad on three separate occasions.

South Africa

In the summer of 2018, after my sophomore year, I traveled to Cape Town, South Africa, for eleven weeks to take part in a Mercer on Mission trip, a service learning-based study abroad program. I interned with a community development organization through the South Africa Internship Program. For three weeks, my Mercer on Mission cohort worked with students from two secondary schools to host a Model United Nations Summit. We were also spread across three primary schools to support English learning in classrooms and observe their school administration and the experiences of students. Once this concluded, I remained in the city and began living with a new cohort of Mercer students while we interned for eight weeks. At Iliso Care Society in Khayelitsha, I supported the organization's social media, marketing, and community outreach work. I worked with a team to coordinate the logistics and facilitation of a government program focused on sexual health and the development of positive self-esteem, and spent time in their early education center.

Upon returning to Mercer for my junior year, I knew I wanted to go back. The opportunity arrived when a group of my friends expressed interest in taking part in the internship program during the spring semester. I embarked on developing a research project with my dear friend, Hinal Patel, to undertake in Cape Town. In thinking about our combined interests and my past experience there, we proposed a project to the Institutional Review Board (IRB) titled, "The Effect of Intergenerational Trauma on Political Activism Among Youth in Post-Apartheid South Africa." Conducting surveys and focus groups in six racially diverse secondary schools in Cape Town, we spoke with 112 students to gauge which factors do or do not push a student to play a politically active role in society.

Through this project, we wanted to learn whether these students, who were born after the end of the apartheid in 1994, were affected by stories from their elders. Specifically, we sought to understand whether apartheid's lasting impact on their families affected their trust in the South African government. By exploring these issues, we hoped our findings could serve as a starting point for youth to use their personal experiences and their families' historical experiences to participate more within their local or national governments.

Mongolia

Shortly after returning from South Africa for the second time, I began preparing to take part in the first Mercer on Mission to Mongolia, under Dr. Jonathan Addleton and Dr. Bryant Harden, in the summer of 2019. Through the program, we spent three weeks working to understand the consequences of unequal, rapid economic development and societal transition in one of the most remote countries in the world. Specifically, our project was to hold an educational summer program for primary school-aged children through the Children of the Peak Sanctuary, a project located in a "ger community" outside of the capital city, Ulaanbaatar.

A ger community is a residential settlement that consists of tented houses, or *gers*, that are easily deconstructed and later reassembled. Those who live in these communities are often Mongolians who have emigrated from the countryside to the urban center of the country in search of better economic opportunities. Instead of receiving said opportunities, these communities are shunted to the outskirts of the growing urban environment, where they experience stark economic inequities, lack of infrastructure, and little access to social programs that could support their wellbeing. During the project, I worked with three other members of my cohort to work on building stronger foundations of English literacy. We improved our understanding of the Mongolian language, culture, and the diverse experiences of the children we were working with.

These three trips transformed my foundational understanding of my identity and perspectives. But more than that, they exposed to me the real-world consequences of public policy, and the diversity, yet interconnectedness, of the global experience.

On an individual level, living abroad for the first time served as a crash course in independence and personal adaptability. These trips instilled in me an unwavering sense of self and an ability to advocate for myself and others. Studying abroad is an immersion into beliefs and practices, languages, and geographies that are different from your own. This may seem intimidating, but this immersion is where the positive impacts of these programs truly live. Despite the occasional discomfort with change, I am grateful for all the good that arose from the hard moments. Without these challenges, I'm not sure I would have confidently relocated to the Washington DC area on my own after graduating from Mercer.

Lessons on Cultural Relativism

Students must interrogate and practice their ability to maintain a culturally relevant lens in understanding many different communities. This involves not making judgments of other cultures based on your own, also known as ethnocentrism*. Instead, every culture and community should be understood and experienced as what and who they are, not as what visitors think they should be.

---

* Barbara Miller, *Cultural Anthropology in a Globalizing World*, 2016.

For example, while racial classifications are a social construct, there are unique, nuanced, legal, and cultural identifications for race that are based on differing historical contexts across the globe. In comparing South Africa and the United States, it is not helpful to apply an American perspective and experience in trying to understand race in South Africa. Despite these categories evolving in recent years, race and ethnicity in the United States are classified under the labels of white, Black, Hispanic/Latino, Asian, and Native American. These titles consistently fall short of capturing the identities of the American people. In South Africa, due to apartheid, the legal classifications—again exclusionary—fall into white, Black, Indian, and Coloured. Due to the historical and present legacies of chattel slavery, Jim Crow laws, and white supremacy broadly, an American may instinctually, and understandably, associate "Coloured" with systemic racism, segregation, and violence. However, in South Africa, this is a racial classification, chosen identity, and valued culture for many South Africans that encompasses a multiracial ethnic community with a deep, complex history[†]. Without this culturally relevant lens, one is unable to develop a meaningful understanding of race and ethnicity in South Africa.

Another significant takeaway from my study abroad experiences was that those who are most likely to be harmed by decisions should be the ones controlling those decisions. These trips were foundational in my belief that there are no academic teachings that should outweigh the expertise of lived experience, especially when it comes to public policy, development projects, research studies, and more. Those affected by an injustice are best equipped to lead their liberation.

[†] Minority Rights Group: "Coloureds—Minority Rights Group," January 20, 2021. https://minorityrights.org/minorities/coloureds/#:~:text=The%20communities%20designated%20as%20coloured,settlers%2C%20and%20from%20other%20Africans.

This understanding emerged from community-led, intentional discussions with those I worked with at Iliso Care Society, the students we spoke with during our research, and those I engaged with in Mongolia. While Hinal and I developed our research study to center on intergenerational trauma's effect on youth political activism, our focus group sessions primarily centered on the failure of the South African government to meet the needs of its constituents. The students discussed inequities that deeply affect their lives and well-being every day, with issues ranging from healthcare to policing to housing. Instead of trying to direct the conversation to meet our initial goals, we saw that we had to step back and let discussions flow organically. We learned that addressing political activism is often not a priority in communities that lack the resources and support needed to meet their basic needs.

Ultimately, we left with more than just "findings" highlighting what South Africans need to thrive, we also left with the invaluable lesson that, as outsiders, we should never presume to know what a community needs. While I knew this academically as a major in international affairs and global development, these experiences were a real moment that could have had real consequences if I did not decenter myself and my assumptions. My study abroad experiences vitally transformed my approach to public policy, research, and development, teaching me to step back and let communities lead.

In a similar vein, studying abroad awakened me to the reality that rights on paper do not automatically translate to rights and freedoms in people's lives. While I experienced and witnessed this constantly in the United States, I had never been pushed to think critically about the idea. During our research, a student shared, "Apartheid has only ended on paper. It is done because there are certain laws in place now. Sure, we can go to whatever beaches and whatnot, but it's still here all around us. We weren't even part of it, but we can see it. We can feel it. We are exposed to it."

While circumstances may vary, this sentiment strikes a chord with many marginalized Americans. Post apartheid, South Africa adopted one of the most progressive constitutions in the world, yet for many South Africans, it is not reflected in their day-to-day lives. Similarly, in the United States, issues like the enduring effects of slavery, the Jim Crow South, the forced displacement of Native Americans, and other atrocities committed against racial minorities and other marginalized groups have not been mitigated beyond paper. Without intentional policies and acknowledgment of harm, such as reparations, many Americans will continue to experience vast inequities and trauma, just as those born into post-apartheid South Africa.

Another example of legal rights that are not prioritized or well-resourced is the constitutional right Mongolian citizens have to a "healthy and safe environment and to be protected against environmental pollution[‡]." Yet Ulaanbaatar is one of the most polluted capitals in the world[§], largely due to those in ger communities having to burn coal to stay warm during the nation's harsh winters. Without broadly addressing the economic inequity in the country's rapid urbanization and specifically addressing the lack of basic infrastructure in these communities, Mongolian people, especially children, are routinely subjected to the devastating health consequences of air pollution.

These real-life experiences—only made possible by studying abroad—allowed me to recognize that legal rights must be implemented as policies designed to acknowledge and combat contemporary inequities rooted in historical violence and trauma. This realization has completely changed how I understand the United States

---

[‡] "University of Minnesota Human Rights Library," n.d. http://hrlibrary.umn.edu/research/mongolia-constitution.html.

[§] UNICEF Mongolia. "Climate Change," n.d. https://www.unicef.org/mongolia/environment-air-pollution.

and, to this day, influences how I work in public policy, take part in advocacy, and engage with different communities.

Lessons on Supporting Communities

My invaluable study abroad experiences taught me that, from local to international levels, power is truly rooted in community. As I wrote during my time in Mongolia, "There is power in numbers. The more people, the more ideas, the louder the collective voice becomes." South Africa has a strong history of activism that is rooted in organizing within communities, as does the United States. Among other struggles, this activism has been linked to the fall of apartheid and to the student-led movement to decolonize the South African education system. In the United States, we have witnessed the legal abolishment of chattel slavery, the growth of the women's suffrage movement, the birth of the Civil Rights Movement, the rise of Black Lives Matter, and more. The power in these movements is rooted in community organizing and advocacy.

Something that has continued to strike me since I visited South Africa is the country's external commitment to solidarity and support. South Africa has been vocal in addressing various African conflicts, the Israeli-Palestinian conflict, and more. To me, this demonstrates that even though South Africa has its unique history, its people have been able to apply their experiences and lessons to support other nations and communities through their struggles. While those who are harmed directly should be leading their struggle, it is valuable for those on the outside to stand in solidarity and allyship. After all, the experiences of the marginalized and oppressed across the globe are interconnected. While every situation is different, it is often possible for people to see themselves in other people and places. I ultimately believe that we are more similar than we are different. Through globalization, there is much to learn from others around the world because, as Fannie Lou Hamer once said, "Nobody's free until everybody's free."

Conclusion

While the lessons and changed perspectives I have written about here are not an exhaustive list, they have had some of the most significant impact on the rest of my undergraduate studies, on how and why I have pursued my chosen career, and even on who I am as a person today. As I mentioned earlier, I do not think I could have relocated for my career without the personal strengths I gained from my study abroad trips. But while I embarked on these trips with good intentions, I was naive, and breaking this naivety completely changed the path of my life. As an example, in South Africa, I was often critical of how the government managed and resourced the public school system, and the subsequent outcomes for the students. However, this criticism was based on a lack of understanding of the nuances of the system and country. In reality, many of my criticisms are the exact ones I would make of the United States.

This kind of reflection and re-learning led to my changing my career goals. With my majors, I wanted to work in international education policy or international development. However, I have since worked in domestic public policy around food systems and security and currently work in early childhood education. In my career as a policy analyst in childcare and early education at national and state levels, my work is largely shaped by what I learned studying abroad. I advocate for policies that center on low-income children and families and Black and brown communities. I analyze policies and practices for their real-world effect on the well-being of those affected. I push for more qualitative research behind these policies and their subsequent implementation to center on the voices and experiences of those most likely to be harmed by them. I explicitly name the historical and present impacts of systemic and institutional racism, white supremacy, and economic and gender inequality in the United States. The implemented policies cannot simply act as temporary Band-Aids. They must directly address and combat the root causes of the marginalization and inequities that exist within different communities.

These internal practices are constantly evolving as I continue to expand my understanding of the history and present conditions of our society and those across the globe. *Studying abroad shaped my understanding that to be a more conscious global citizen and advocate, one must never stop personal learning and growth.*

Seven years ago, I was convinced I had to leave the only place I had ever known to better embrace my own identity and to immerse myself in the diverse communities, languages, and cultures that comprise the rest of the world. Writing this today, I can wholeheartedly say that I was correct. As I have been reflecting on my travel journals, I am still identifying new moments and lessons that have ultimately influenced my life. I am bearing witness to my individual growth and changes that have continued to evolve from then to now and will continue in the future. *I have become a more self-assured, open-minded, and analytical version of myself. In studying race in the United States and South Africa and experiencing more diverse communities, I have continued to become more settled in my own multiracial identity.* In my first-ever journal entry leading up to my first trip to South Africa, I wrote the following: "I only expect knowing that I will not leave South Africa as the same person who landed there, and, to me, that is exciting. I hope to grow, mature, and become a more well-rounded world citizen, and, in general, a better human. I know I will be pushed out of my comfort zone, and I will be pushed to my limits, but that is how I will evolve."

Looking back at the version of me who wrote that, I see that I have since been, and always will be, in a journey of transformation. My opportunities to study abroad during my undergraduate studies were the catalyst.

As a first-generation university student, these opportunities, and the financial and logistical support Mercer University provided to make them possible, shaped an undergraduate experience I never could have imagined. Even now, almost four years after graduation, this experience continues to affect me, both personally and professionally. The opportunity to live, work, or study abroad, along with the intentional decision to make it as meaningful as possible, holds the potential for immediate and lasting effects on your life. I believe these lifelong effects are the greatest takeaways of all. In my last journal entry from Mongolia, I wrote, "This is the sort of experience that you reflect on for the rest of your life." And, truly, it has been.

STRATEGIES FOR LEVERAGING THE TRANSFORMATIVE IMPACT OF STUDY ABROAD

21

PREPARING INTERNATIONAL EXPERIENTIAL EDUCATION TRIPS FOR TRANSFORMATIVE IMPACT

Dr. Mary Alice Morgan

My assignment in this chapter is to share observations on conceptualizing, designing, and executing effectual international experiential education and service learning programs. The goal is to provide helpful suggestions to fellow faculty members interested in teaching a study abroad or Mercer on Mission (MOM) course. The suggestions I share come from personal reflection having co-led nine MOM trips to South Africa with Dr. Eimad Houry and one with Dr. Amy Nichols-Belo, from working with MOM director Dr. Craig McMahan on his advisory committee in the early years of MOM, and from my leading service learning at Mercer as senior vice provost of service learning for thirteen years.

The field of international education has exploded in the past twenty years. It has moved from an old model of students studying abroad as a culturally privileged "finishing" experience to a theorized discipline emphasizing not only cultural exchange but also an examination of global power dynamics and informed, respectful, and genuine intercultural exchange. Today's international experiential education goes far beyond learning a bit about the history or language of a country and then compiling selfies as you work through a list of notable tourist sights (fun though those selfies are).

It is within this framework that I offer the observations below. I encourage readers to consult the many excellent books being written on the subject of global learning. In the space allotted here, I cannot address the important and complex subjects of cross-cultural communication, the typical phases of studying abroad, or cultural humility. Rather, I've focused on three key aspects of planning a study abroad course, and along the way, I share practical "trouble-shooting" tips that I don't see discussed explicitly in the scholarly literature.

I want to say at the outset that study abroad experiences are turbo-charged learning. You can accomplish more teaching and students do more learning in a compact timeframe than our semester-long stateside courses. My tips are as follows:

1. Clearly articulate and target your course learning objectives and assignments.

As faculty, we routinely state course goals for our stateside courses, and students usually have a clear sense of how our courses fit within our general education curriculum or their major. I am assuming that every faculty member leading study abroad provides students with a thorough introduction to the foreign country they will be going to.

But when it comes to studying abroad, it helps to know that students sometimes see the travel and the cultural immersion themselves as the goals of the course. Therefore, they may balk at having those evening debriefing discussion sessions after a full day of work or our journaling assignments or research essays to write. Can't we faculty just <u>see</u> how engaged they are by the transformational foreign experiences they're having? (Yes, we can—but we need to understand how you're integrating and applying your new knowledge.)

Therefore, from the beginning, I encourage faculty to pose questions to your students that help them identify and unpack what they're learning. Here are a few examples:

a. What cultural features of your international locale differ from those in the US, and can you explain the differences in each place from a structural or sociopolitical point of view? For example, what socioeconomic structures do you observe and how did they come about? Do you see evidence of a historical colonial mentality or postcolonial environment?

b. What kinds of intersectional identities do you see within the culture? What roles and status do women occupy? Are there racial hierarchies? What about LGBTQ community members? Who is privileged and who isn't? How does that play out in different individuals' lives?

c. What is the government structure and how is it similar to or different from American electoral democracy? Who has power and who doesn't? How are human rights protected or not protected?

d. What value systems do you see regarding natural resources? Are they protected or exploited?

e. Are there aspects of this country's culture that you wish the US would adopt? What could we in the US learn from this country?

f. How might you change your habits or make plans for the future that will enable you to improve global conditions or ameliorate global problems?

Questions like these not only help students to be observant and understand the new country they are in but also encourage them to consider American sociopolitical structures and value systems from a new revelatory, defamiliarized perspective. It's also true that the goals for your course may be specific to applied learning and therefore not familiar ones for your students. For Mercer on Mission courses, for example, Dr. McMahan encourages faculty to link their work to the United Nations Sustainable Development Goals (SDGs). Approaching coursework from this perspective may require laying the groundwork for students.

2. Selecting and Working with Community Partners

This is mostly for MOM programs or applied learning courses. My advice on selecting and working with community partners is threefold:

—Invest in Mutual Planning

Pairing the skills and benefits our undergraduate students can provide to community partners in international settings takes considerable investigation of potential partners—especially when scout trips may not be available. I cannot stress enough how important it is to invest in mutual planning upfront. You and your community partner should be partners. You should not be asking an organization to incur expenses or completely change its practices for the sake of our convenience in implementing a project. That said, faculty should also be aware that partners are, understandably, often eager for any support that they see on the horizon and therefore may overpromise and underdeliver.

Another key element is to examine what motives or assumptions underlie our work. A memorable shorthand way of expressing distinctions in ways of working within a community is to ask: are our interactions "doing to," "doing for," or "doing with"? On paper, the distinctions seem pretty obvious. But in practice, unconscious or subconscious attitudes can sabotage the mutuality that characterizes "doing with."

"Doing to" is an instrumental, transactional (lack of) relationship. Faculty leaders and students may have an attitude that they are there to "fix" some problem within the community and are eager to implement their knowledge and skills. Students may view community members as needy recipients of their expert knowledge or assets, never considering that our technology may not be sustainable or that our practices may violate cultural norms.

"Doing for" operates from a position of charity and assumes that community members are helpless to contribute to solving their problems. Emphasis is on completing a "do-gooder" task rather than involving and empowering community members.

"Doing with" recognizes and respects the value of the insider knowledge and culture that community members possess and takes the time to co-plan and build trust and mutuality—not just with the community organizer but with those likely to be affected by the project. "Doing with" also usually includes some planning for the sustainability of the project versus one-time volunteer projects.

—Create Clear Agreements

Ask questions about every detail in your plans. We may not be cognizant of details in the international site that would impede our best-laid plans—for instance, rolling electricity blackouts or unreliable transportation times due to breakdowns of busses. Detailed Memorandum of Understanding (MOUs) should be drawn up to prevent problems or misunderstandings.

But be aware that even the agreements in carefully drawn-up MOUs may go awry. So, to the extent that you can, expect the unexpected.

—Prepare Students to be Flexible

Let students know ahead of time that your course won't have the predictability that they've come to expect from courses on our campus and that you expect their flexibility and ingenuity when the unpredicted happens.

Preparing students to be resourceful and resilient is also a good idea. Dr. Amy Nichols-Belo incorporated teamwork training and leadership training into a MOM we co-led. Not only did this help the students understand our high expectations of them, but when our community partner misunderstood our request that we offer a workshop for four groups of twenty-five and instead sent all one hundred participants to us at once, our students did not panic. They used their training to turn to one another, and in five minutes they had divvied up the duties they were to accomplish, established a rotation, and carried on (though in a din of more than a hundred voices).

3. Assessing Learning and Assessing Impact

I have never encountered a student who studied abroad or participated in a MOM who says they didn't learn much. For students, these are genuinely life-changing experiences. We've captured some of those effects in the essays in this volume. Another measure of learning and outcome is the number of Mercer students who go into careers dealing with international affairs, global health, global development studies, international business, and various kinds of international service. The growing number of MOMs being offered at Mercer and the growing number of students studying with our partner universities abroad are a third index.

Compared to those growing numbers, it may be harder to assess the learning and results of studying abroad outside the confines of the learning objectives and specific assignments in our courses. One course may stress language acquisition and proficiency. Another may emphasize intercultural awareness. A third might focus on global challenges to social justice or environmental issues.

Fortunately, in the past ten years, the field of international education has developed extensive lists of learning objectives that can best be called "global competencies." Faculty members wishing to identify nuanced learning objectives such as the three below can consult lists like the one linked below from the University of Michigan:

- Understands the complexity and interconnectedness of global processes, such as environment, trade, and human health, and can critically analyze them as well as compare and contrast them across different cultures and contexts.
- Develops a personal sense of ethics, service, and civic responsibility that informs their decision-making about social and global issues.
- Recognizes the influence of cultural norms, customs, and traditions on communication and uses this knowledge to enhance their validity.*

Finally, though this is not part of my graded assessments, I think that asking students to self-report what they've learned—in journal entries throughout the course and/or in a reflection essay at the end of the course—is an important opportunity to give them. While we as faculty members can measure intellectual or even attitudinal learning through assignments, only students can know the interpersonal growth or challenges they are experiencing. In my experience, asking students when they felt most tested by our work in our international community, when they felt most connected to the community members, what they learned from or hated about working in teams, what they will tell their parents about the trip...these questions have elicited responses that have often surprised me in their depth of self-knowledge and growth. The practice of journaling can also help support students in managing their emotions as they encounter unfamiliar situations that may precipitate grief, self-

---

* P. Roy, E. Wandschneider, & I. Steglitz. (2014) Assessing Education Abroad Outcomes: A Review of the BEVI, IDI, and GPI. White Paper. East Lansing: Michigan State University Office of Study Abroad.

recrimination, anger, or a sense of inadequacy or helplessness in the face of the issues to which they are contributing.

To conclude, I cannot overstate the value that global education opportunities offer students (and their professors). But beyond these, global education offers benefits worldwide, both in terms of learning about global interdependence and rich cultural differences.

22

CREATING ENDURING IMPACT THROUGH INTEGRATIVE LEARNING APPROACHES

Dr. Eimad Houry

The integrative learning approach encourages students to make explicit connections between different disciplines by integrating knowledge from a wide range of academic fields.* In the field of international affairs, integrative learning entails making connections between disciplines such as economics, history, religion, anthropology, and women and gender studies among others. Understanding complex national and global challenges is a daunting task by any measure, and an interdisciplinary approach informed by critical tools such as diverse worldviews, linguistic proficiency, and intercultural competency is indispensable. Despite this challenge, when executed efficiently, integration holds important learning outcomes for students. Research has shown that students who are part of integrative studies programs can apply new learning to their lives, analyze diverse perspectives, and demonstrate a greater ability to comprehend and interrogate nuances within complex contexts.† The value of integrative learning cannot be overstated. It is increasingly considered an important skill for addressing the world's complex challenges.‡

---

* J. B. Leonard. (2012). "Integrative Learning: A Grounded Theory." *Issues in Integrative Studies* 30:48–74.

† Leonard, 2012.

‡ D. Bok. (2006). *Our Underachieving Colleges: A Candid Look at How Much Students Learn and Why They Should Be Learning More.* Princeton, NJ: Princeton University Press; A. Gutmann. (November 17, 2005). Educating for Citizenship:

Arguably, what sets integrative learning apart from other interdisciplinary modes of discovery is the experiential element. Broadly speaking, this usually refers to study abroad programs, but as evidenced by the essays in this volume, service abroad is a more profound and effective tool in achieving an enduring effect on students. Service work abroad is one of the most effective ways to promote global interconnectedness among students. Through service, students quickly realize that many of the challenges facing developing societies, and the ways they are trying to manage them, are not too different from similar challenges faced at home. Students also come to learn that the lack of solutions is often not because of a dearth of ideas but because of limited resources that impose constraints on what can be accomplished and at what pace. What sets integrative learning apart is the application of knowledge, either through more nuanced and sophisticated discourse or through service to others.

Assessment is one of the most challenging aspects of evaluating the value of integrative learning. In the following section, I share strategies I have used within this approach to enhance student learning as well as foster the integration of knowledge and experience gained.

Directed Advising

Leveraging the value of studying abroad is an intentional process that unfolds in stages. When a student meets with me to discuss their interest in studying abroad, the first question I ask has nothing to do with the destination but more to do with the student's career aspirations. We then discuss topical interests, career goals, and future study plans. I usually let the student know that going abroad is only the beginning and that during and upon returning we should meet to discuss ways to harness the benefits of the experience.

Locally and Globally. Keynote presented at the 30th Annual Conference of the Association for the Study of Higher Education. Philadelphia, PA.

I have used several ways and tools to help students extract value from studying abroad. The most obvious one is to begin with the choice of courses to complete during the study abroad period. If an internship is involved, I encourage students to be intentional about doing research, preferably using the work site and location to collect original data. I require them to turn in midterm and end-of-term reports reflecting on their experiences and describing what they believe they took away from the experiences they had.

Follow-up advising and conversations are crucial elements in capturing and harnessing the actual impact of studying or working abroad. These exchanges take on several forms, including maintaining ties with hosts after returning to the US, meeting with students (often at my urging) to explore ways to capitalize and build on the value of having gone abroad to a specific destination, and, in some instances, encouraging students to form student groups to help plan and continue supporting host organizations we learned about and sometimes worked with while in the country.

Once the student returns, we discuss internships, scholarships, summer programs, and other opportunities, both on and off the campus. However, leveraging study abroad for career-related decisions is by far the trickiest and most challenging to accomplish.

Among the student contributors, several were selected to serve as Fulbright scholars, Peace Corps volunteers, or fellows. Successfully competing for these programs was no accident, and there is no doubt that having studied abroad was a pivotal piece of the package. For each of these opportunities, students spoke at length about the formative impact of having traveled and lived abroad and how the lessons they picked up along the way influenced their career decisions and the direction they took afterwards.

Program-Related Strategies

Integrated Planning

Specific meetings, visits, and partners should be selected and included in a way that reinforces the academic goals of the program. Not only does this provide a better context, it also leaves a more lasting impact, as evidenced by student journal entries and the academic and career decisions that follow.

Research-Based Immersive Learning

Every program I led also included a research component that allowed participants to think more deeply and critically about a specific aspect of the country or encounters. Several students later refined the research assignments for presentation at regional, national, and international academic conferences.

Student Documentation of Learning

We cannot assume that students will derive meaning from their experiences. Faculty must work diligently to cultivate those thoughts and to ensure that students are learning what they should from their experiences. To do so, my colleague and I would require students to journal throughout the trip. We collect journals regularly, write extensive feedback (often by way of asking more questions!), and then meet with the individual students to discuss their entries.

No matter the approach, having a plan to help students integrate knowledge acquired through immersive learning experiences is key. While all trips abroad hold the potential to benefit students, they still need to be plugged into supportive academic programs and contexts that foster the integration of learning that took place abroad. It is within such supportive environments that deep learning and the transformative impact of the exposure can indeed be leveraged.

23

REFLECTION:
A HIGH-IMPACT PRACTICE OF SUCCESSFUL TRIPS ABROAD

Dr. Chinekwu Obidoa

Study abroad programs feature a constellation of activities that provide opportunities for deep learning for students.* However, we cannot take deep learning or growth from exposure to life in a foreign setting for granted. Deliberate effort needs to be made to embed strategies into the study abroad program that enable students draw meaningfully from their experiences. Such strategies ensure that students maximize the likelihood of leveraging the multidimensional impact of the experience.

Academic discourse on the impact of study abroad trips includes the application of several theories, among which is the Experiential Learning Theory (ELT). The ELT developed by Kolb in 1984 posits that to maximize learning, the learner must immerse themselves fully, without reservation, in new experiences and also reflect on their experiences from diverse perspectives.† They also need to be able to create ideas that combine their findings with broader theories and subsequently use those theories for decision-

* R. M. Gonyea, The Impact of Study Abroad on Senior Year Engagement. Paper presented at the annual meeting of the Association for the Study of Higher Education, Jacksonville, FL, November 2008.

† David Kolb (1984). Experiential Learning: Experience as the Source of Learning and Development.

making.[‡] This process enables the learner to take actions that usher in transformation.[§] Hence critical reflection plays a central role in facilitating transformative impact through immersive learning experiences.[**]

The Merriam-Webster Dictionary defines reflection as "a thought, idea, or opinion formed or a remark made as a result of meditation." It usually involves intentional and directed thought or contemplation on a specific topic, scenario, encounter, or context and calls for a quiet, careful, and sometimes systematic consideration of facts, arguments, perspectives, and opinions surrounding a subject matter. As a verb, synonyms of "reflection" include speculate, deliberate, cogitate, reason, and think.

Reflection can be invited with a prompt embodied in a question, a picture, a debate, a dilemma, or even conflict.

The goal of reflection is to emerge with a refined understanding or new illumination, a new sense of direction concerning the subject engaged. Connecting the dots between complicated concepts and seemingly contradictory realities is by no means a mediocre benefit of reflection.

Reflection draws heavily from personal knowledge but quickly advances to accessing ancillary knowledge, depending on the factors on which it is anchored, such as the inclusion of the thoughts and ideas of others and the timeframe provided of the exercise. Reflection can be done individually or collectively as a group.

[‡] Kolb, 1984.

[§] H. Strange and H. J. Gibson. (2017). "An Investigation of Experiential and Transformative Learning in Study Abroad Programs." *Frontiers: The Interdisciplinary Journal of Study Abroad* 24/1: 85–100. https://frontiersjournal.org/wp-content/uploads/2017 /04/XXIX-1-STRANGE-GIBSON-TransformativeLearningPotentialof-StudyAbroad.pdf.

[**] S. L. Ash & Clayton, P. H. (2019). Generating, deepening, and documenting learning: The power of critical reflection in applied learning.

For all the faculty-led trips I have organized, I have found the practice of reflection invaluable in cementing and capturing student learning. In the following section, I share how I incorporate this practice in my trips.

Daily Reflection

I build a daily reflection session into the itinerary of every trip. I create a block of time in which I anticipate minimal or no form of disruption for this exercise. I also ensure that it takes place in a space void of external distractions. This is a requirement for all students and is communicated during the pre-departure lectures. It is considered "a sacred" part of the trip, and failing to attend, participate, or show up on time can be considered a "crime." These sessions can take place in the quiet side of a hotel lobby just after breakfast or before we place orders for a sit-down meal at a restaurant. They can also be held outdoors in spaces that allow for maximum engagement and conversation. A session usually starts with a prompt to which each student is expected to respond. The discussion usually unfolds as students share their thoughts and perspectives.

Prompts can be based on the academic subject matter on which the trip is based or on topics on personal or professional growth. Here is an example of a prompt inviting reflection in the area of personal and professional growth: "Share something that resonated with you from your activities of the day and connect it with something from your past, your present, and your future."

Invariably, this invitation to think about their current experiences and how they connect to who they are, and possibly who they hope to become, allows the experience to be centered more poignantly on their lives, stripping it of invalidity and obscurity.

Prompts relating to academic subject matter can be drawn from lectures, interactions with hosts and locals, moments of tension, or new knowledge acquired within the new cultural setting.

Blog Reflection

Students are required to write and submit three blog reflection entries during my short-term faculty-led trips. A virtual blog site is created for the class where students can submit their blog entries. The entries are reflections on different aspects of knowledge gained and/or experiences during the trip about the course topic.

Post-Trip Reflection

As part of the course requirements, each student is required to write a final reflection essay which is usually a one-page (single-spaced) reflection on their overall experience. The essay includes personal and professional insights and takeaways from the trip. A longer essay may be more desirable, but other course assessments are also due at the end of the trip. A succinct reflection is sufficient for capturing and summarizing personal and professional learning.

There are many other ways to embed reflection into a study abroad trip. For instance, some of my colleagues use personal journaling and diary entries to capture student learning during trips. In this format, students are expected to write daily or intermittently in their journals. I witnessed the beauty of this form of reflection during the Mercer on Mission trip to Mongolia in which I participated. The lead professor of the trip, Dr. Bryant Harden, ensured that each student acquired a personal journal and completed twenty reflection entries before the trip was over. While students complained about the tedious task, I was moved by the quality of their questions and comments during group discussions. Such depth of reflection cannot be dissociated from the individual reflection that was required of each student through journaling.

Also, the variety and depth of post-trip reflection can be more expansive to include specific and directed questions regarding selected cornerstone student learning outcomes of a course or trip. For instance, for their post-trip reflection essay for the Mercer on

Mission trip to South Africa, Dr. Eimad Houry and Dr. Mary Alice Morgan required students to respond to these prompts:

"Compare your awareness of disparities in health and social development before you participated in this trip with your current impressions. What have you learned about the developing world? About being American?"

"Reflect on how this experience may have changed the way that you see yourself and the world. What has this global engagement affirmed about your sense of self and the world and what has it challenged, morally, spiritually, ethically, and politically?"

"At Mercer, we often talk about a sense of calling and purpose in the world. Has this experience inspired or changed your sense of what you are called to do in the world? Reflect on whether your experience will change your actions in the future. If so, how? If not, why not?"

These types of directed questions to well-articulated learning outcomes encourage students to reflect on specific aspects of their learning and experiences abroad. This helps students make explicit connections with past knowledge and perspectives. Answers to such questions provide a stepping stone for them in their effort to leverage the impact of what they have experienced.[††]

There are many ways to design reflective exercises for study abroad programs to maximize their transformative power.[‡‡]

In whichever form it takes, reflection provides invaluable benefits for students, including the following:

[††] Ash and Clayton, 2009.

[‡‡] J. Eyler, D. E. Giles, and A. Schmiede. (1996). A Practitioner's Guide to Reflection in Service-Learning. Nashville, TN: Vanderbilt University; R. G. Bringle and J. A. Hatcher. (1999). Reflection in Service-Learning: Making Meaning of Experience. *Educational Horizons* 7/4: 179–85, 1996.; E. Zlotkowski and P. Clayton. (2005, April). Reclaiming reflection. Paper presented at the meeting of the Gulf South Summit on Service-Learning and Civic Engagement. Cocoa Beach, FL, for features of high-quality reflection exercises.

- Helps them make connections between past learning and current learning
- Allows students to challenge stereotypes and make meaningful connections across concepts, disciplines, and contexts
- Ushers in deeper and full-circle understanding of concepts or course content
- Helps with the clarification and sense-making of past learning
- Catalyzes personal and professional growth
- Builds oral communication skills
- Assists in identity formation
- Helps to grow personal confidence
- Invites the ability to dream or imagine a different world for themselves
- Facilitates and supports personal accountability
- Affirms growth of psychological traits such as empathy, caring, and cultural relativism
- Aids perspective forming and conviction building
- Ushers students into the "reflective practice," which is a relentless learning process where individuals critically reflect on their attitudes and actions to spur ongoing adaptations in various areas of personal and professional life

None of the personal or professional growth reported by students featured in this book would have been possible without their engaging in the practice of reflection. Reflection facilitates self-discovery, lifestyle change, discovery of purpose and calling, advancement in career development, further travel, self-discovery, and deep learning, as recorded by these students.

I have developed, led, co-led, and participated in trips abroad to seven of the eight world regions. Irrespective of the type and duration of the trip, I have observed the manifestation of all these benefits of deep reflection in the lives of students.

In summary, reflection is invaluable in helping to extract student learning while abroad. Without proper and meaningful documentation and sharing of new knowledge gained as well as the preservation of such information through reflective writing, it is difficult to capture the impact of a study abroad trip in its entirety. More importantly, reflection before, during, and post-trip helps set the stage for students to be able to leverage the impact of the trip when they return.

24

A JOURNEY AS THE COORDINATOR OF MERCER UNIVERSITY'S SERVICE LEARNING AND INTERNSHIP PROGRAM IN CAPE TOWN, SOUTH AFRICA

Anwar Parker

Introduction

I have always been passionate about promoting diversity and making positive changes in communities. As a psychologist, I've spent a significant part of my career working in community development and mental health programs in South Africa, and student service work often seemed to be closely aligned with my main goals. My association with Mercer University commenced in 2008. I vividly recall meeting Dr. Craig McMahan, the director of Mercer on Mission, during his scouting mission to South Africa in 2007. As I guided him through our diverse array of community, health, and youth projects, our discussions brimmed with shared enthusiasm, innovative ideas, and possibilities. We spoke about the intricacies of the Cape Town context and the potential for positive change. We also spoke about the profound impact of experiential learning on students. We explored the transformative power that immersion into new contexts and engaging in dialogue with diverse individuals hold, challenging preconceived stereotypes and notions. It was a dialogue that underscored the significance of hands-on experiences in broadening perspectives and fostering a deeper understanding of the world, and this laid the foundation for what would evolve into an enduring collaboration. A few months later, Mercer University manifested its commitment by dispatching the inaugural cohort of service learning students to South Africa, led by Dr. Mary Alice Morgan and Dr. Eimad Houry. Little did I know at that moment that this initiative would not only blossom into a regular service-learning project but would also culminate in the establishment of a comprehensive internship program for Mercer students. This evolving partnership with the faculty has since flourished into a deep and lasting friendship, extending over decades.

As the South African coordinator of this program, I assumed a multifaceted role that encompassed the preparation of students for the unique South African context, securing suitable partnerships and placement sites, addressing challenges through effective troubleshooting, and facilitating coaching and debriefing sessions with the students. This essay offers my insights into the organizational dynamics of study abroad programs through collaborative efforts with our partners in South Africa. I also hope to convey the enormous impact that it has had both on communities and on the students during their service in Cape Town.

Preparing Students for the South African Context

Cape Town is a city marked by its diversity and complexity and compounded by numerous socioeconomic challenges. Much of its current landscape is a product of the apartheid era, and understanding how the legacy of apartheid continues to influence the city's dynamics is an intricate task. It necessitates a profound understanding of the forces that shape change, the context in which these changes occur, and the cultural sensitivities that play a pivotal role in navigating this terrain.

Many students were venturing abroad for the very first time and possessed limited knowledge of the South African context. To bridge this knowledge gap, we meticulously designed pre-departure orientations. These seminars were focused on understanding South

African culture, delving into its historical depths, and grasping the dynamics of its social fabric. They also equipped students with the tools necessary for meaningful engagement. Historical briefings laid the groundwork for understanding the roots of the challenges faced by the community, and discussions on social responsibility instilled a sense of ethical commitment.

For example, a key component of one of the service learning project's orientations involved an in-depth examination of the lingering impact of apartheid on education in South Africa. By analyzing case studies and engaging with local educators, students gained insight into the challenges faced by the education system and explored avenues for positive contributions during their time abroad. This proactive approach helped them not only understand the historical context but also develop a sense of responsibility toward addressing present-day issues in the education and schooling system.

Finding Appropriate Placements

The success of any service learning and internship program hinges on the careful selection of placements that align with students' academic pursuits and personal goals. The process involves more than just matching resumes with job descriptions; it requires the establishment of robust partnerships with local organizations. These partnerships need to be meticulously curated to ensure that placements meet academic requirements while simultaneously making a meaningful impact on the community. We actively sought partnerships with a diverse range of stakeholders, from NGOs and businesses to governmental bodies. This deliberate diversity of opportunities allowed us to create a symbiotic relationship where students not only thrived in their academic and professional pursuits but also made tangible contributions to the host organizations and the community at large.

Placement sourcing did not always go smoothly. Potential host organizations had a spectrum of views on accepting international student services. Some eagerly opened their doors, recognizing the value of fresh perspectives and the potential to fill critical skills gaps. These forward-thinking organizations saw the international students as catalysts for innovation and positive change.

On the flip side, there were those hesitant hosts, skeptical about the contributions international students could make within the context of their organizations. Concerns ranged from fears of language barriers to worries about students' safety or that students might need excessive support. My role became pivotal by brokering understanding and clarifying expectations on both ends. The success of these programs necessitated a nuanced understanding of the local dynamics and a commitment to fostering relationships that transcended borders, contributing positively to both the educational journey of the students and the community's growth.

Troubleshooting and Support

In the face of meticulously planned initiatives, it became clear that challenges were an inherent part of the process. These obstacles could range from interpersonal conflicts and unforeseen cultural shocks to unexpected logistical hurdles and mismatched expectations. My role expanded beyond initial planning to encompass troubleshooting and timely support.

An example of some troubleshooting involved a situation where a student, despite pre-departure orientation, found it challenging to assimilate into the new cultural context. This manifested in difficulties in communication, understanding local norms, and navigating social dynamics. It left the student feeling overwhelmed and unhappy. This required me to step in to address these challenges by facilitating a cultural sensitivity discussion, providing additional support through conversations with the host organization, and encouraging open dialogue among participants to foster a more inclusive environment.

Coaching and Debriefing

Facilitating the transformative journey of students was not just a responsibility but a genuine privilege. By incorporating regular coaching sessions, we were able to create a platform for reflective learning, allowing students to bridge the gap between academic knowledge and real-world experiences. The process enhanced their understanding and nurtured a more profound connection to their educational pursuits.

Furthermore, recognizing the significance of individual experiences, I went beyond group debriefs by scheduling personalized sessions for each intern. These one-on-one debriefs delved into the nuances of cultural immersion and encouraged interns to share their unique perspectives and challenges. Students were often encouraged to confront and challenge their preconceptions. This deliberate effort aimed to create an environment where students gained practical skills and also underwent personal growth.

Regular debriefing sessions also played a crucial role in helping me understand the specific support that students required. By offering students the opportunity to talk freely, we gained valuable insights into their needs and concerns, allowing us to tailor our support more effectively. Detecting potential challenges early on is essential for addressing issues promptly and ensuring a positive and supportive learning environment for all students.

Collaboration with Partners

The foundation of a thriving study abroad program lies in a robust collaboration with local partners. We soon realized importance of establishing crystal-clear expectations, maintaining consistent communication, and cultivating a shared sense of responsibility. This laid the groundwork for a sustainable and mutually beneficial relationship. Respecting the local context was a guiding principle throughout the collaboration. This meant that cultural nuances were acknowledged and program elements needed to be actively adapted based on feedback from local partners.

The most important quality for international service projects engaging with communities in other countries is humility. Humility in this context means acknowledging and respecting the local community's knowledge, customs, and experiences. It involves approaching the project with an open mind, recognizing that the community members are experts in their own lives and have unique insights that should be valued. This ethos of humility promotes a partnership-based approach where everyone involved, including faculty and students, learns from one another.

Impact on Students

The influence of the service learning and internship program manifested prominently in the transformed perspectives of our students, constituting a source of immense gratification. It made me happy to see how much their perspectives changed, and hearing about the lessons that they were learning. The change observed in these students often included a profound metamorphosis in their identities as global citizens. The testimonials of many students in the program demonstrated a deepening cultural empathy, heightened awareness of social issues, and an appreciation for the transformative potential of experiential learning.

I remember one student who was fixated on her grade for the course and saw the experience as primarily an academic pursuit. Initially, she viewed her role through a lens of academic duty. However, through direct interaction with the local community, understanding the challenges faced, and actively participating in grassroots initiatives, the student underwent a paradigm shift. This shift transcended academic knowledge, and she developed a profound cultural empathy as she connected with the daily realities of the community, realizing the human stories behind the statistics.

A heightened awareness of social issues emerged as a recurring theme among students. Unlike traditional classroom settings, the immersive nature of service learning and internships provides a dynamic and real-world context for applying theoretical knowledge. Students recognized that the transformative impact on their perspectives was not solely derived from textbooks but from actively engaging with diverse communities, adapting to unforeseen challenges, and developing practical skills that transcended the academic realm.

These collective impressions prove the enduring value of international study programs in shaping well-rounded individuals poised to contribute meaningfully to a globalized world. Beyond academic achievements, the program succeeded in cultivating a sense of responsibility, empathy, and adaptability among students—qualities essential for navigating an interconnected and diverse global landscape. In essence, the impact of such initiatives extends far beyond the classroom, leaving a mark on the character and worldview of the participating students.

Being a part of their growth has been an extraordinary honor and privilege, allowing me to contribute, in my small way, to their development. Moreover, the profound friendships cultivated throughout this journey are a source of everlasting gratitude, enriching the experience and making this a truly cherished chapter in my life.

CLOSURE: LEVERAGING THE IMPACT OF EXPERIENCES ABROAD

You are now back from your study abroad trip. You have shared thousands of pictures with friends and family on your social media pages. You have spent what now seems like close to a hundred hours sharing stories with friends, family, classmates, and anyone who had time to spare about your amazing trip. Without a doubt you had a blast, you learned a lot and you truly feel your life has changed! Now what? What next? What do you do with all you now know and the person you feel you have become? What do you do about the fire you strongly believe has been ignited in you? How do you maintain and sustain the change you experienced? Basically, how do you leverage the impact of the experience? You cannot take the experiences you had for granted. What you learned will not automatically translate to great impact without concerted effort on your part. In this chapter, we share some ideas on how to think about the impact of your study abroad experience, as well as some practical steps to make the most of those experiences. These tips and strategies were gleaned from the stories shared in this volume.

Setting the Stage: While You Are Abroad

• Remember that your goal and strategy to ensure the long-term impact of your trip abroad starts while you are abroad. You will need to be intentional about how you document, capture, and preserve your learning so you have something to work on upon your return.

• Seek ways to connect your existing interests and ideas with your trip abroad. While abroad, explore connections with specific topics and issues (academic and personal) you are passionate about within and beyond the focus of the class or program.

• Pay attention to the growth that is taking place within you.

Creating Momentum: Within the First Months of Return

• Seek more knowledge about issues you were exposed to abroad; there is always a lot more to learn about any subject matter.

• Take time to engage in a deep and critical reflection of your encounters. Sit with the discomfort and contradictions you were exposed to for longer than a few minutes. This will help you examine, sift, and analyze what you want to keep and incorporate into your life.

• Don't lose the fire that was ignited in you. Find a project into which you can channel the newfound ideas, energy, and desires that you gained abroad. You can easily lose the growth that comes from discomfort if it is not channeled into a project or task that brings meaning and a sense of purpose.

• Seek to have the critical questions that emerged during your time abroad answered. Ask more questions, and make the pursuit of those answers your mission even if they end up being a lifelong pursuit.

• Seek ways to make connections between what you have been exposed to and other learning opportunities when you return.

• Build on new skills acquired. This can include language skills, hobbies, and technical and academic skills.

• Take new classes that help you learn more or build on new learning and interests. If such classes do not exist, you can work with your advisor, department, or any professor to develop an independent study that will help you continue your journey of learning.

• Explore new opportunities for internships and fellowships to build on new ideas and areas of interest.

• Determine to work on areas of weakness in your life highlighted during your time abroad. This may include enlisting in further language study to learn a new language.

• Maintain contact with people you met during your time abroad.

• Read your reflection essays and journal entries about your experiences abroad over and over again. This is an important form of reflection that should help you develop lasting strategies for growth from your experiences abroad.

Sustaining Momentum: Cementing Transformation Months and Years after Return

• Don't stifle the emergence of a new you even if it is a drastic personality change. As long as it is positive, don't be ashamed to emerge into the new person you have become. This includes embracing your changed perspectives about the world, the country of your birth, and yourself.

• Seek groups that do similar work you were exposed to abroad and in which you became interested, and join their mission. For example, many students are exposed to social inequality abroad and return with a newfound understanding of how inequality works. If you find yourself in this category, find ways to participate in programs that disrupt poverty, injustice, and marginalization in the US when you return. Regardless of the topic or issue, make a concerted effort to find and connect with groups on campus or organizations in the country that focus on work you now value as you continue your journey of learning and growth.

• Be courageous when making big decisions concerning your life, no matter how daring—even if it means leaving home again. It is possible that what you experienced was just the tip of the iceberg and that the pull you feel is evidence that there is more to be seen, known, and to become. Several of the students featured in this book recognized the need to return abroad after their first trip. For many of them, the second and third time abroad served to consolidate and cement the learning and transformation that they encountered during their first time abroad. Putting off returning abroad or further engagement abroad may delay or hinder your ability to maximize the newfound ideas and areas of personal growth that can be facilitated in such a setting. You also don't want to be haunted by wondering what life could have been if you had traveled again.

• Be courageous to take the next step and make the change you feel led to make in your career journey. This may mean retraining for a new career path or exploring new career options.

• Share with people how your experiences abroad transformed your life.

While this list is not exhaustive, it is a starting point and serves as a springboard for further action. Altogether, it sets you on a path toward deep change, which is an undeniable requirement for changing the world; the world changes as we change.